REAL-WORLD WHITETAIL BEHAVIOR

REVISED EDITION

JIM ROY

THE DERRYDALE PRESS
Lanham and New York

THE DERRYDALE PRESS

Published in the United States of America by
The Derrydale Press
A Member of the Rowman & Littlefield Publishing Group
4501 Forbes Boulevard, Suite 200, Lanham, Maryland 20706

Distributed by NATIONAL BOOK NETWORK, INC.

First Derrydale paperback edition 2003

Library of Congress Control Number: 2003100546
ISBN: 1-58667-098-0 (alk. Paper)

∞™ The paper used in this publication meets the minimum requirements of American National Standard for Information Sciences—Permanence of Paper for Printed Library Materials, ANSI/NISO Z39.48–1992. Manufactured in the United States of America.

TABLE OF CONTENTS

DEDICATION

To my wife, Gayle; to my children, Kim, Kenny, and Kelly. And to the living memory of Fred Bear.

ACKNOWLEDGMENTS

I would like to thank my family and all my friends who helped make this book possible. Especially, Angela Haggins, Chief Librarian of the Smithsonian Environmental Research Center, a good friend who provided me with much assistance in locating and obtaining research materials for my studies; Dr. James Lynch, environmental research scientist and friend; Daniel Murphy, D.V.M.; and Mr. Y. Kirtpatrick-Howat of Contee Farms.

EDITOR'S FOREWORD

When Jim Roy submitted his manuscript to our publisher, Doug Mauldin, it included an author's note that began "Most of the people who will be reading this book have probably never heard of Jim Roy . . ." I don't know about most of the people, but *I* had never heard of Jim Roy. That's too bad, because I'm fast approaching middle age (some folks would say I'm there already!), and there are a whole bunch of things about whitetail deer in this book that I wish I'd understood—in the simple and clear way Jim explains them—a long, long time ago.

There are reasons why you and I haven't heard of Jim Roy—at least, not until now. Jim hasn't been spending his time writing articles about whitetails. Instead he's been out in the woods studying—and hunting—whitetail deer. In fact, as you'll find as you read Jim's book, he doesn't have much time for "outdoor writers" like me. After reading his book—several times now—I have to agree with him. There's more knowledge and know-how on whitetail deer crammed into these pages than I have ever read in any one place.

You'll also find that Jim Roy is outspoken and opinionated—a luxury that he's earned the right to. He has strong feelings about what works, based entirely on what has worked for him over a lifetime of hunting and studying whitetail deer. Although I'm certainly no whitetail expert—nor, I fear, the caliber of hunter that Jim Roy is—I would give you the one *caveat* that Jim himself admits to: His hunting has been mostly in the hard-hunted, heavily pressured, heavily wooded eastern region. You, therefore, may not agree with everything you read here. You don't have to agree, and you certainly don't have to follow Jim's recipes for success . . . recipes that have worked for him time and again in what are almost certainly some of the most difficult hunting conditions throughout the vast whitetail range. But I *know* you'll be fascinated. And I know you'll say to yourself—repeatedly— "Why didn't I think of that!"

Jim Roy hasn't come to his conclusions—or revelations—either by accident or through bolts of lightning. Rather, the knowledge contained in this book has come from a lifetime of serious study. *Serious* is a good word, for Jim Roy is the most serious and most dedicated whitetail nut I've encountered. Some of you will probably think him mad . . . and at the very least he's mad about whitetail deer!

A skilled bowhunter since before he was a teenager, Jim Roy served as a reconnaissance team leader in Vietnam—served quite well, by the way—and got himself badly shot up in the process. When he came back home he returned to his eastern woods and hollows—and has literally spent the last quarter century hunting the whitetail deer when it was legal and studying him when it was not. He considers himself a professional bowhunter and a whitetail behaviorist, and I reckon he's earned both titles. As a bowhunter he's taken some eighty-five trophy-class whitetail bucks—most of them from his eastern woods, mountains, and hollows. As a student of whitetail behavior, he spent twenty years working for the Smithsonian Institute at an Environmental Research Center.

This research center, located on the western shore of Chesapeake Bay, was a haven of abandoned farmlands, forests, rivers, streams, and marshlands that contained a few herds of native, free-ranging whitetail deer. Unlike so many studies, Jim had the unique opportunity to study native, wild, completely natural whitetail deer in their natural habitat—habitat that was relatively undisturbed and unhunted over a twenty-year period.

Unlike so many students of wildlife behavior, especially today, Jim Roy always approached his study with a hunter's eye. As he studied "his" deer, watching them, trapping them, tagging them, testing buck lures and antler rattling and so much more, he came to believe that much of what he had read about whitetail deer and whitetail hunting was simply not true. Although he had already been a successful bowhunter, he changed his tactics as he learned . . . and his hunting got better.

In 1977 and 1985 he won the National Field Archery Association "Diamond Buck Award" for the largest whitetail deer taken in North America by bow in those years . . . and he was runner-up between 1979 and 1984. This with bucks from the East, not the Canadian giants you read about! Twenty-seven of his bucks have dressed out over 200 pounds . . . also from the hard-hunted East. In this book he stresses hunting tactics and whitetail knowledge, but I suspect he's a pretty fair stick with his bow. He's a many-time state champion in the instinctive shooting archery class, and holds the current record for the Maryland Archery Association's State Broadhead Championship in the bowhunter division. He's been a hunting adviser for Precision Shooting Equipment, and, putting his whitetail knowledge to art, has been a taxidermist for more than twenty years.

Impressed? You should be. Interested? You should be. I'm actually a bit awestruck by the knowledge and insight in this volume. And, to tell you the truth, I was a bit skeptical. It all started with a phone call from Doug Mauldin, who said he had received, out of the blue, an interesting manuscript from a fella named Jim Roy. "Never heard of him," said I. But I'm grateful for the opportunity to read and reread his book . . . and you will be, too.

And now, I must offer to you and to Jim Roy that which an editor never does: an apology. Jim wrote this book without chapter breaks, from start to finish, intending to draw his readers through the whole process and not tempt them to read it chapter by chapter. The chapter breaks and headings are mine, not his, made essential for placement of our color photos and to maintain the consistency of this volume within our Whitetail Secrets series. As an editor I had no choice . . . but as a reader, I hope that you'll do as Jim Roy intended and read this book from front cover to back. I suspect you'll do that more than once. As a hunter, I know you'll find a whole new trove of "whitetail secrets" with each reading!

Craig Boddington
Paso Robles, California

INTRODUCTION

For as long as I can remember I have been listening to people talk about whitetail deer and how to hunt them. Some people seem to believe that success in deer hunting is strictly a matter of pure luck, being at the right place at the right time. Some people read everything they can get their hands on about the whitetail deer and claim to know everything there is to know about whitetails and how to hunt them. But week after week, year after year, these same people return home from the woods with nothing to show or tell—except excuses. Could it be possible that these people have been listening to and reading bad information all these years? Could it be possible that these people just do not know how to hunt? I think it is a combination of both reasons.

Modern man has never really learned to hunt! He has never had to! Ever since the early 1900's most people have either purchased their table meats from butcher shops or grocery stores, or raised their own livestock. Commercial meat sources replaced modern man's basic need to hunt meat to survive, and hunting deer became a sport. When "survival hunting" disappeared from man's daily life so did a lot of the "old world" hunting skills and knowledge. They were replaced by hunting clubs and hunting stories. People still hunted for deer, but their reasons for hunting changed, as did their methods.

Deer hunting became a yearly vacation for many people. It became their reason for taking a refreshing break away from life's daily routine and the city lights for a while. They could see the mountains, walk through the woods, and smell the fresh outdoor air. And maybe, if they were really lucky, they might even bag a deer while they were out hunting with their fathers or grandfathers or a few of their friends. At night, on the way home or sitting around a campfire, they told their hunting stories.

Deer hunting became a social event rather than survival. Hunting stories became modern man's "Law of Nature," and the primitive, simple survival-type of hunting was lost. And that is what this book is all about: a simple, common sense method of hunting that I call "survival hunting." It begins by learning "Real-World Whitetail Behavior."

Jim Roy
Berkeley Springs, West Virginia

CHAPTER ONE

HERD DYNAMICS AND MOVEMENT

"To kill a deer, you must know the ways of the deer!" In this first section of the book, I will try to unravel, and explain, some of the mysteries and myths concerning the whitetail deer. I will be discussing deer, their normal behavior, and their normal movement patterns under "natural conditions," by which I mean unpressured situations. No humans or dogs, etc., forcing the deer to move. So, sit back, relax, and let your mind learn and understand the life habits of the whitetail deer.

Deer are herd animals, and creatures of habit. Their survival is dependent on these facts. Knowing and understanding their habits as well as they do is the true secret to hunting them.

All deer live as members of some herd. The number of deer within any herd varies, but all deer herds consist of *family groups*, which are *parental does* with *fawns*, and *individuals*, which are lone bucks and single does of various ages. And, there could be many different, separate, small herds of deer living in any given area of land that is large enough to support them.

All deer, at birth, begin their lives in small, social units, called family groups, controlled by their mother, a doe. This parental doe teaches her fawns everything they need to know to live and survive as individuals and as herd members.

Fawns are born in late spring, a time of the year when the weather is mild, and the forage is plentiful. Two fawns of either sex is considered to be the normal litter size. However, a doe could birth from zero to four fawns, all depending on the availability of specific food sources in the area where they live. If a doe did not consume the right combinations of various and specific food sources while she was pregnant in early winter, the doe would either abort the embryos to save precious energy, or reabsorb the embryos to gain additional energy to survive the winter. If a doe consumed plenty of the right combinations of specific foods, she could give birth to four fawns. This is one of nature's methods of controlling the population of deer in the wild, when there are not enough food sources in the area to support more deer.

Fawns remain with their parental doe throughout the summer, fall, and harsh winter, all the time learning and experiencing life as nature had planned. Fawns are physically rejected away from their family group by their parental doe, if she is pregnant, near the end of their first year of life. This usually occurs in mid-spring, just prior to the upcoming birthing season. Parental does that did not mate, or became pregnant during the previous mating season or rut, will usually keep their now one-year-old fawns, called *yearlings*, with them for companionship and safety throughout the summer and early fall, until the rut begins to occur again. Then the yearlings, now a year and a half old, are driven away from the family group and their parental doe by the very aggressive, much larger, breeding bucks of the herd when they look for and single out the does of the herd for mating. Either way, the fawns are now yearlings. They have experienced the worst of all the seasons of the year, and now they must live and survive as individuals within the herd.

Whitetail deer are very territorial, as individuals and as a herd. Their survival is dependent on how well they know the territory or land they live on. Most deer will generally travel and spend their entire lives in, a small well-defined area of land, called a *home range area.* The actual shape and size of an individual deer's home range area vary greatly, depending on the terrain, the locations of food and water, and cover. Deer, or any other animal in nature, will not spend any more energy than absolutely necessary to obtain food, water, and cover. Therefore, an individual deer's home range area is simply defined to be the minimum amount of traveling distance on an area of land that contains enough food, water, and cover to survive. In most cases, at least in the East, it is generally considered to be less than one square mile in area, per each prevailing wind direction. One individual deer's home range area could be two hundred yards wide by three miles long, while another deer's home range is a quarter-mile wide by two miles long, per each prevailing wind direction.

Fawns share their mother's home range area during the first year of their life. Then after being rejected from their family group, they each establish their own home range area, branching off from and overlapping their mother's home range area. This is how nature directs young deer to remain in their parental doe's herd, by keeping them near their mother's scent in the herd's home range territory.

The total area of land encompassing all the home range areas of all the family groups and individual deer of the entire herd is called the herd's *home range territory.* Just how large a section of land a herd's home range territory covers depends on the season of the year, the terrain, and the number of deer in the herd. Within any deer herd's home range territory, the individual deer and family groups belonging to that herd share and have overlapping home range areas with other members of that herd. This is the basis to the deer herd's defense system. If any one deer of the herd is disturbed while it beds, feeds, or travels anywhere within its home range area or the herd's home range territory, its reactions alert the rest of the herd.

A deer herd's home range territory in mountainous regions is generally much larger than that of a deer herd located in flat, farmland areas. This is for the simple reason that deer living in mountainous regions usually have to travel much greater distances to locate the seasonal food varieties, water, bedding, and cover areas.

Deer live as herd animals, and they bed as herd animals. The most dominant deer of the herd, usually the larger bucks, take the best bedding sites, and the rest of the herd bed out away and around them at various distances and locations.

The age, physical size, and aggressiveness of each individual deer establishes its dominance ranking or "pecking order position" within the herd, or among other deer. Yearlings begin their lives as individual deer at the bottom of the dominance ladder. The older, larger individual deer of the herd control where, and just how close in distance the younger individual deer bed, feed, and travel near them. It is strictly a function of one deer's tolerance of another deer's presence, and it varies greatly at different times of a year. A large, mature, herd buck may not allow another individual deer or a family group to bed within 100 yards of him. A family group controlled by a very large, older parental doe may not allow any other family groups or individual deer of the same herd to bed within forty yards of her. Whitetail deer are considered to be mature animals at three and a half years of age.

All deer herds consist of family groups and individuals.

The individual deer and family groups bedded down throughout the herd's home range territory all function as "listening posts" for the rest of the herd. Their bedding behavior and reactions alert the rest of the herd to any approaching danger. This bedding arrangement is a "security screen" that protects the entire herd, especially the breeding stock, the herd's mature bucks. This is a typical deer herd defense system, designed by nature, and that is why big, mature whitetail bucks are hard to hunt. They are protected by the herd! Sometimes these herd bedding sites cover a vast area of land, all depending on the terrain, the direction of the wind, the size of the deer herd, and the time of year.

The direction of deer travel within any deer's home range area, or the herd's home range territory is controlled daily by the direction of the wind. Deer movement itself is triggered by daylight conditions. Daylight is the key to deer life, as it is for just about everything else on this earth. The length of day in sunlight time and its intensity, called "photoperiodism," are what controls the deer's movement and

Whitetail fawns are born in late spring, a time of the year when the weather is mild and forage plentiful.

biological behavior. The winds and the weather control where the deer travel to feed and bed.

In the late afternoon, the sun begins to fall on its setting path. This slowly lowers the light levels or intensity of daylight on the land. Deer sense the diminishing light levels through the dilating pupils in their eyes, and whenever the lowering light conditions reach a certain trigger point, the deer randomly begin to rise from their beds and start their feeding activity. The entire deer herd does not rise from their beds and move out toward their feeding grounds all at once. It is a slow, methodical process that begins with the herd's family groups and the other less dominant individual deer, which are bedded down in and around the outer fringes of the herd's bedding area, moving out and away from the bedding area first. These deer function like "scouts" for the rest of the herd. If they are not disturbed as they travel out through the herd's home range territory in their home range areas, they are followed in time by the

A nice buck bedded in his daytime bed, not always in heavy cover but always where he can take advantage of the wind currents.

slightly more dominant deer of the herd, followed some time later by the larger, more mature bucks of the herd. Should anything disturb any one of the family groups or individuals as they travel, the rest of the herd would be alerted to the danger and nothing would follow.

To better understand how a deer herd beds and moves away from its bedding area, imagine yourself perched 1000 feet above the earth, looking down on a deer herd's bedding area, without any leaves or treetops blocking your view of the land below. Try to visualize in your mind, or draw on paper, four family groups of deer and three individual deer all bedded down in a circular pattern at various distances away from each other, all around one, mature herd buck bedded down on a small hilltop located somewhere in the center of the herd's bedding area.

Now, imagine a slight wind blowing across the deer

herd's bedding area and daylight levels dropping in later afternoon. Then visualize the family groups, at slightly different times, rising from their beds and walking off in the same general direction as the wind, moving out to some imaginary feeding area. Now, visualize the three individual deer, some time later, rising from their beds in some random order and following the family groups' travels, each on their own separate trail leading to the same feeding area. Then, visualize the herd's mature buck, later in time, rising from his bed and following the travel of the three individual deer, on his own separate trail leading to the same feeding area. This is basically how most all whitetail deer herds bed and move out from their bedding areas, no matter where they are located.

The only variables to this example of deer movement would be the amount of deer involved, the terrain, and the time frame between when the first deer of the herd rises from its bed to feed and when the most dominant deer of the herd actually leave their bedding areas. Once again, this is all controlled by "photoperiodism," the direction of the wind, and each deer's "pecking order position" within the herd.

Generally, on clear to partly cloudy days most deer begin rising from their daytime beds about three hours before dark, and they usually return to their daytime bedding areas within three hours after sunrise. The most dominant deer of the herd usually do not leave their daytime bedding areas until well after dark, and they usually return to their daytime beds well before daylight. Their learned, life experiences have taught them to move only under the cover of darkness.

On dark, cloudy days, the continuous, lower-than-normal, daylight conditions stimulate the deer to rise from their beds much earlier in the afternoon, and bed down much later in the morning.

Mature bucks are the last to leave the herd's bedding area—often just at dark as this buck is doing.

The full moon affects all things in nature, especially deer movement behavior. On clear to partly cloudy days, during the ascending and descending days of the full moon, deer rise from their daytime beds much later than normal, and bed down much earlier than normal. The bright moonlight provides slightly higher than normal levels of light at sunset and sunrise, which create a "twilight condition" on the land and in the woods, and it takes longer than normal for natural light levels to fall to certain trigger points to stimulate the deer to react. Most deer, during the full moon, usually do not leave their bedding areas until just before dark or later, and they usually return to their bedding areas well before sunrise.

One of the most misunderstood facts about whitetail deer behavior is how deer use the wind. Most hunters would bet their best "cold weather boots" that deer always travel with their nose in the wind. Not so! Under "natural conditions" deer travel in the same general direction as the wind. This is commonly called "wind to their back."

Ever since the beginning of time, whitetail deer have been chased and hunted down from behind by predators. As a defensive measure to help prevent a surprise attack from the rear, deer instinctively learned to bed, feed, and travel with the wind at their backs, or quartering off of their backs. Quartering off their backs means that the wind flows across the deer's back, more from the side than from the rear. In doing so, the scent of any predator approaching the deer from their rear, hundred of feet or yards away, would be carried to the deer's nose by the wind long before it ever arrived to harm them. Deer constantly, effortlessly, *scent-check* the winds that carry scents from distances behind them as they bed, feed, or travel, by simply lifting their noses to the air occasionally, or side to side as they walk.

Deer usually enter crop fields and other open feeding areas from the woods, with the wind to their backs or quartering off their backs. They trust their eyes and ears to protect their front and sides as they travel through the woods and enter into open areas, and they use the wind to protect their back. By doing so, anything moving toward the deer through or from the woods that the deer have just safely passed through traveling with the wind to their backs, would be nosed by the deer long before it ever arrived. Anything approaching the deer from their front or sides, or from across the open area as they enter, feed, or travel through the open area, would usually be heard or seen by the deer long before they would ever be threatened. This is why deer usually feed their way out toward the middle of crop fields and other open areas to feed and many times to bed for the day. With the wind protecting their backs, and their eyes and ears protecting their fronts and sides, most deer are virtually unapproachable without detection. A family group of deer bedded down somewhere in the middle of a large field of tall corn within the herd's home range

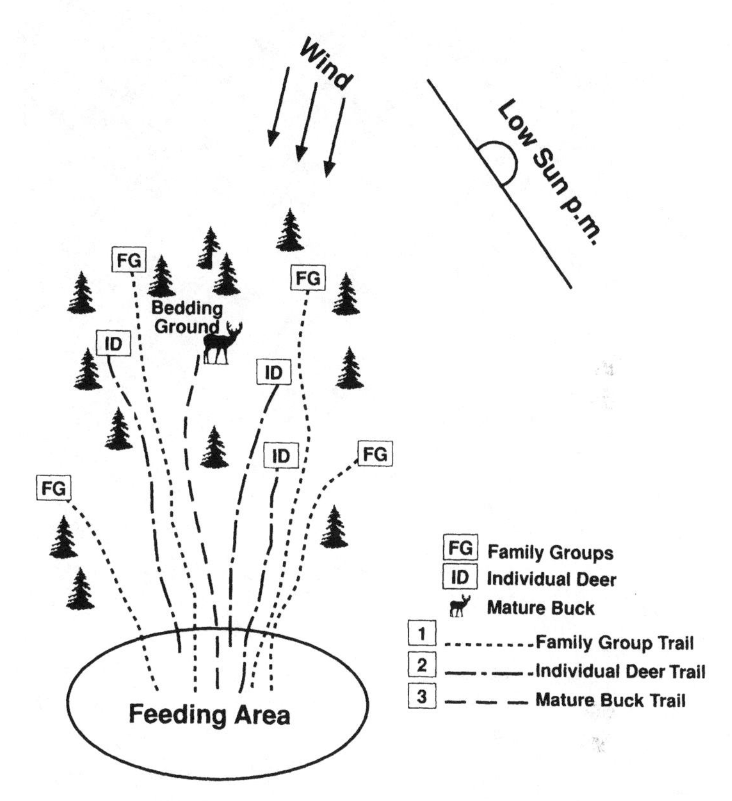

In the evening, deer leave their bedding areas randomly but in 1 2 3 order.

territory, is just as safe, if not more so, than deer bedded down in the middle of the woods on a side of the mountain.

Deer will usually only turn their noses directly into the wind when they want to *scent-locate* something, such as a strange noise, a bowhunter up a tree, baited areas, a *scrape*, etc. Deer scent-locate the objects of their attention by walking out around the object at some safe distance downwind,

Whitetail deer usually enter crop fields and other open feeding areas from the woods, with the wind to their backs or quartering off their backs.

called *circling*, until they cross the object's scent path. If their curiosity is excited downwind, they will usually follow the scent path, with their noses into the wind, right to the source. If they are alarmed by the scent path downwind, they will travel away from it, with the wind to their back or quartering off their back.

Many times when an individual deer or family group of deer begin to cross a road, and they are caught by surprise in the middle of the road by an approaching vehicle, they will turn and run back in the same direction they just came from. This happens because the deer believe it is safe to run back to where they have just safely come from. The deer have been traveling with the wind to their backs, so they know nothing is following them. The deer have not seen or heard anything to spook them, up until they began crossing the road. The deer are unsure of what may await them on the other side of the road, so they instinctively turn their noses into the wind, and travel back to where they know it is safe.

Most times when deer that are following other deer across a road get caught by surprise in the middle of a road after one deer has already safely crossed, the others will usually try to follow across the road. The deer have been traveling with the wind to their backs, so they know nothing is following them. The deer just watched another family group member or another individual deer of the herd safely cross the road in front of them, so the deer believe it is safe to follow and they do. Both of these situations are normal deer behavior, and that is why some deer run out in front of traffic and why others run back across in front of traffic.

CHAPTER TWO

AIR CURRENTS AND DEER MOVEMENT

Deer usually circle out around their bedding areas to scent-check the area from somewhere downwind before they ever approach their daytime beds, and they enter their bedding areas with the wind to their backs. Deer lie in their beds with the wind to their backs, and leave their beds with the wind to their backs or quartering off their backs. Once again, deer rely on their eyes and ears to watch their front and sides, and they let the wind protect their rear.

Deer always select their bed sites according to the direction of the wind, and climatic conditions. A bedding area used by deer on a sunny day, controlled by southerly winds, would not be used on cloudy days during northwest winds. Just as a bedding area used by deer during southeast winds would not be used when westerly winds prevailed.

On days when there is very little wind or none at all, *air thermals* control where deer bed, feed, and travel. Air thermals are soft currents of air that slowly rise or fall as the result of the temperature of air. Warm air rises and cool air falls. Air thermals rise and fall with the sun, and deer travel up or down with the air thermals.

As the sun rises on clear to partly cloudy days, it slowly heats up the cool, nighttime air and causes it to slowly rise.

This sun-heated warm air, or *warm air thermals*, rise upward toward the sky all day long, until the sun begins to set in late afternoon. Then the air slowly cools down, and gently falls back down toward the earth as *cool air thermals*. This cool air falls all night long, and gently flows down into and through all the low areas of land like an invisible fog. This cool air thermal condition remains until the sun warms the air again and causes it to rise.

When the sun begins to warm up these cool air thermals again, a condition called a *thermal reversal* occurs and stops the cool air from falling. During the thermal reversal, the temperature of the cool air becomes too warm to continue falling. It reaches a point of neutral buoyancy and completely stops flowing for four to five minutes, until the sun warms the air a couple of degrees higher and causes the air to begin rising. Thermal reversals occur each time the thermal air currents change their direction of flow up or down, normally twice a day—once in the morning and once in the late afternoon. However, on damp, cloudy days or rainy days there are no thermal reversals. The damp or wet air is just too dense or heavy to rise. The thick layers of cloud cover block out the sun and prevent the sun's warming rays from drying out the air. So it continues to flow down into and through all the low areas of land all day long, like nighttime cool air thermals. Just like fog, cool air thermals remain until the sun burns them off.

All of nature is affected by thermal reversals and the sudden stillness of air. The entire forest becomes totally silent. Birds stop singing, insects and small animals become quiet and remain very still until the thermal reversal is completed. Deer change their direction of travel, up or down, to high or low ground areas, after a thermal reversal occurs.

If you ever happen to be up high on the side of a mountain before daylight, stop moving for a couple of minutes and you will feel the soft cool air thermals flowing against your face as you look up toward the top of the mountain. Once the sun begins to rise, stop moving again and sit down, looking down toward the bottom of the mountain, and wait for the thermal reversal to occur. Now you will feel the falling cool air thermals on the back of your neck. Soon after the sun rises, you will feel the cool flow of air on the back of your neck suddenly stop. You will hear the entire woods become totally quiet for the four to five minutes it takes for the thermal reversal to be completed. Then, you will begin to feel the warm air thermals rising up from below, against your face, and you will begin to hear the birds and insects once again. You really need to experience a thermal reversal this way to better understand how *thermal reversals* work, and how and why deer movement is controlled by them.

Over large, flat areas of open land air thermals normally flow up or down between the ground and the sky. But in hilly or mountainous areas air thermals flow up or down through the draws in the sides of the hills and mountains. Draws are the large, vertical cuts or depressions in the sides of hills and mountains that feed up from the bottomlands or valleys below. Draws function like giant air ducts or troughs between the high and low areas of ground, with currents of air being funneled up or down through them. In some areas, draws are called cuts, drainages, hollows, etc.

On sunny to partly cloudy days, most deer living in mountainous regions usually bed in the flat, saddle areas near the sides of draws to take advantage of the warm air thermals rising up through them. The larger, more dominant deer of the herd take the best bed sites near the tops of the highest draws, and the rest of the herd bed out and below them at various distances. Draws are narrow at the top and wide at the bottom, and when a herd of deer is bedded down along both sides of a draw, the herd's bedding arrangement roughly resembles the shape of a triangle. This is a perfect, defensive bedding situation, designed by nature to protect the herd's mature, breeding bucks that are bedded down above the rest of the herd.

From these high bed sites, deer effortlessly scent-check the rising warm air thermals and all the odors carried up with them from below. Should a hunter or predator walk through the bottomlands below or step into a draw 200 or 300 feet or yards below a bedded deer, their scent would be carried right up to the deer's nose by the rising warm air thermals. Any deer bedded down above would be alerted to the danger moving around below them, and would be gone long before they could ever be approached or threatened.

A herd of deer may use one very large draw to bed in or two to three different, smaller draws running parallel to each other on the same side of the mountain. Many times a small herd of deer will bed above or directly across from another small herd of deer that is bedded in a different, parallel draw on the same side of the mountain and use the other herd's bedding behavior to warn them of any approaching danger. It all depends on the number of deer in each herd, the size of the hill or mountain, and the size of each herd's home range territory.

After the thermal reversal occurs in the late afternoon and cool air thermals begin to fall, deer begin traveling in the direction of the falling cool air thermals—down. Deer move down into the low areas of the herd's home range territory, traveling with the falling thermal air currents to their backs just as they use the wind. Anything approaching the deer from behind as they move down to feed would be scented long before it ever arrived to harm them. Once

Thermals

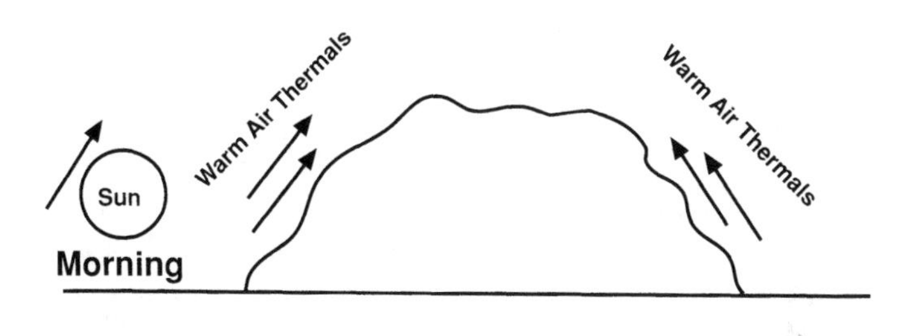

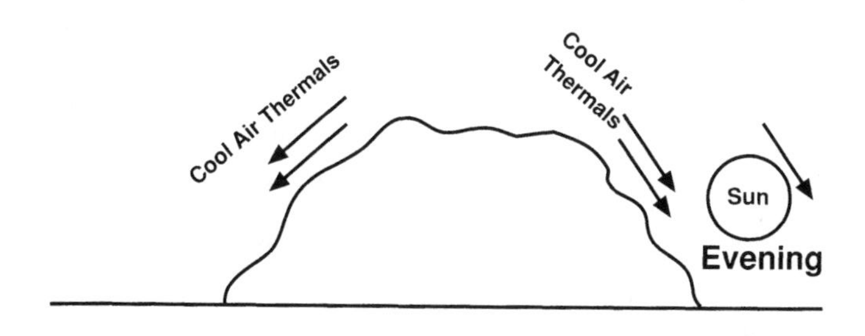

again, the deer use their eyes and ears to detect danger to their front and sides and use the falling cool air thermals to protect their rear.

Deer travel with the nighttime cool air thermals to their backs or quartering off their backs all night long or until the next thermal reversal occurs. Then they use the rising warm air thermals to their backs as they move back up to the higher points of the herd's home range territory to bed.

Deer living in the mountainous regions usually travel up or down the sides of draws using the falling or rising air thermals to their backs as they move to and from bedding and feeding areas. Lowland deer usually travel in more circular patterns.

On sunny to partly cloudy days, deer that live in the lower, more flat regions of land usually bed down on the highest points of land found within their herd's home range territory, to take advantage of the rising warm air thermals. Once again, the larger, more dominant deer of the herd bed down on the highest points of ground and the rest of the herd beds out, around, and below them.

On dark, overcast days or rainy days, deer living in all areas bed down in the lowest areas of their herd's home range territory to take advantage of falling cool air thermals. The scent of any hunter traveling around on higher ground any distance above them would be carried right down to the deer. They would be alerted to the danger moving above, and the deer would be gone long before they could ever be threatened. Deer remain in these low ground or bottomland areas to bed and feed until the sun dries out and warms the air again and reverses the flow of thermal air currents.

Regardless of their environment, all deer use thermal air currents when there is no wind and sometimes in combination with the wind. Remember these facts about air thermals and deer. On clear to partly cloudy days, deer bed in high areas. On cloudy, rainy days, deer bed in low areas. Deer move to higher ground after the thermal reversal occurs in the morning, and they move to lower ground after the thermal reversal occurs in late afternoon. There are no thermal reversals on damp, cloudy, or rainy days, and deer remain in the low ground areas to bed and feed until the next thermal reversal occurs.

Many times, on sunny to partly cloudy days, deer will bed down in *blow-down areas*, found on the sides of draws or other high ground areas of the herd's home range territory. Blow-downs are small areas of land in the open woods, where trees are constantly being blown down by

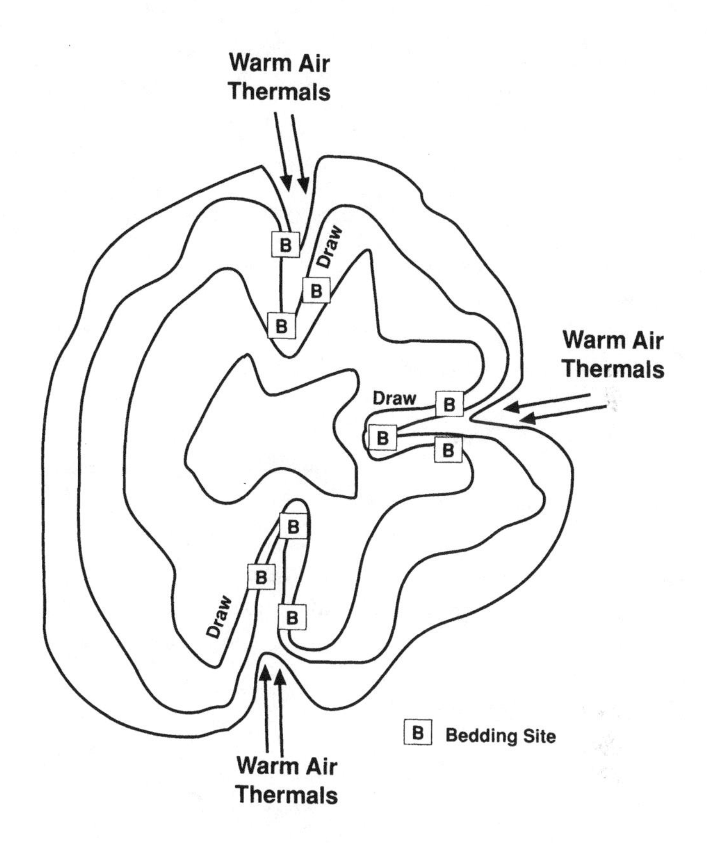

Through the day, warm air thermals carry scent up draws to bedding sites; in the evening after the thermal reversal, deer travel down the sides of draws to low ground areas with the cool air thermals to their backs.

strong winds. Deer usually bed down beside the trunks and branches of the fallen trees that lie all over the ground throughout these types of areas. The fallen tree trunks and branches provide the deer an open type of concealment that partially hides their bodies, yet allows them to have good visibility of the open woods around them.

From these high ground blow-downs the deer are able to look over large areas of land to watch for movements in the woods below or around them as they bed. The deer are able to hear most any disturbance and detect the scent of any hunter or predator moving through the bottomlands below by using the rising warm air thermals. And, most times, should a hunter or predator attempt to approach the bedded deer from or through the open woods all around the blow-down, the loud crackling and snapping of dead branches under the hunter's feet as the hunter walked near would definitely alert the deer long before they could ever be threatened. Nature could not have planned it any better!

During the cool or cold, sunny days of fall and winter, deer usually bed down in the blow-down areas, clear-cut areas, and other open thicket areas that are directly exposed to the sun. They bed down on the sides of draws, the ridges of mountains, and slopes of land that have southern exposure to the sun. Like most other animals in the wild, deer burn off much of their stored body fat just trying to stay warm in cold weather. By sleeping directly in the sun's warming rays, deer save precious calories of energy that they may need later on to survive during times of heavy snows, when many necessary foods are covered. Many times during cold weather the deer will leave their beds in the morning sun near mid-day and travel across the ridge of a mountain, following the sun from one side of the mountain to the other side to bed down in the afternoon sun.

During periods of heavy rain, snow, or very strong winds, deer usually bed down in areas of thick cover. Dense pine forests, greenbriar thickets, large patches of honeysuckle, and other types of these areas are typically good *cover areas* for deer. They all provide deer with shelter from the elements, sources of food, and safe bedding. Deer also use these types of cover areas to escape and hide safely

A doe in her daytime bed. The family groups and then the younger bucks will literally surround the herd's mature bucks, making their beds virtually impregnable.

from dogs, hunting pressure, etc. The direction of the prevailing wind each day determines which cover areas the deer use.

Deer usually will not venture too far from their cover areas during times of strong, gusting winds. The winds, blowing hard and shifting directions, create an unstable situation for deer and other animals in the woods. The shifting air currents, with leaves blowing and swirling across the ground and old, dead limbs and branches breaking off trees and falling to the ground, all create sounds and disturbances that put a deer's nervous system into a state of frenzy. Generally, deer will not leave their cover areas until the winds have settled down somewhat and stabilized directionally. However, after three days of continuous rain or wind most deer will temporarily leave their cover areas for other sources of food or water and to stretch their legs. Then they usually return to their cover areas until the storm is over. I have witnessed this situation many times while hunting bear, deer, and moose.

The only normal exception to the whitetail deer's bedding behavior that I have previously described to you would be during the periods of extreme heat and drought that sometimes occur in late summer and early fall. During these times, deer and many other animals will usually bed down in the shaded, cooler sections of draws or bottomland areas that are located near sources of water in the herd's home range territory to escape the direct rays of the sun and its searing heat. In these particular bedding situations, many times the deer are trading their safety for comfort. However, while they are bedded down the deer will use the thermals or wind to their best advantage!

During the night, deer occasionally bed down to rest and chew their cuds. These random, temporary, nighttime bed sites are usually located in open feeding areas, and they are also selected according to the direction of the wind or thermals.

Deer have three basic modes of behavior: *normal*, *alert*, and *spooked*. A deer's normal behavior is how it acts and survives under "natural conditions." The alert or alarmed mode is how the deer reacts when it senses that something is wrong. The spooked mode is when the deer panics and runs away.

Deer have three senses that hunters have to contend with: sight, hearing, and smell. Deer are primarily nocturnal animals. They feed and travel mostly during the darkness of night. The deer's large eyes provide them with excellent vision during the darkness of night, and the ability to easily detect movement. However, during the hours

Whitetail deer use their eyes and ears to watch their front and sides, while the wind coming from behind protects their rear.

of daylight, deer can see no better than humans, as far as I am concerned. What they see, I can see!

Deer have large, pivoting ears which provide them with a longer range of hearing and the ability to sound-locate the sources of noise. Deer hear things at much greater distances than humans, but they do not hear any better at close distances, as far as I am concerned. What they hear, I can hear!

The deer's sense of smell is really the most important thing that hunters must be concerned about. A deer's entire life is controlled by its nose. They recognize their food, their young, danger, and most everything else primarily by their sense of smell. If you can fool the deer's nose, you can kill the deer! I will discuss how to do this later on in the book. Right now, it is more important to learn and understand how deer use their eyes, ears, and nose together.

When any one of the deer's senses is triggered, it enters into an alarm-like state of mind. This alerts the deer that something is wrong or out of place. Deer do not usually panic or run while they are in this alert mode of behavior. They will either become very curious or very cautious, and that all depends on each individual deer's age and its own life experiences.

It takes two of the deer's senses, triggered in any combination, to cause the deer to spook and run. For example, if a deer heard you snap a branch under your foot as you stalked in toward it for a closer bow shot, the deer would be alerted to a noise and freeze in place. Then it would watch for any movement, and scent-check the wind for any strange odor in the air. If no movement was seen by the deer, and no foreign odor was detected after a few minutes of intense concentration, the deer would slowly relax, and continue on with its activity. If the deer saw any movement at all, the second sense would have been triggered, and the deer would panic and run without any hesitation whatsoever. If the deer heard something and scented something, it would spook and run. One sense alarms! Two senses panic!

If a deer sees something that is out of place, and it is unable to scent it or hear it, the deer would usually try a variety of tactics to cause that object to move. It may alternately stamp one, or both, of its front feet hard to the ground as it slowly approaches. Or, it may slowly lower its head to the ground, as if it was about to feed, only to snap its head back up quickly to try to catch the object in movement or to see if the object has moved. Eventually, it will try to circle out around the object at some safe distance, until it reaches the object's scent path downwind. Once the deer scent-locates the object downwind, it will either spook or follow the scent path right to the source.

Generally, regardless of how long it takes, an alarmed deer will not relax, or continue on with its normal activity, until it discovers the source of its alarm. However, deer that instantly recognize the familiar scents, shapes, or sounds of danger do not need their second sense to be triggered before they spook and run. Their own previous life experiences have instinctively taught and conditioned them to react in panic to the scents and sounds that they associate with danger. Naturally, they spook and run!

CHAPTER THREE

SCENTS, SOUNDS, AND THE RUT

Deer communicate and recognize other deer primarily by the use of three external sets of glands located on each deer's body: the *interdigital glands*, the *metatarsal glands*, and the *tarsal glands*.

The interdigital glands are located between the hooves on all four feet of the deer. As a deer walks, trots, or runs, it deposits scent on the ground wherever it travels. Each time a deer's foot lands on the ground, the interdigital gland of that foot leaves a small amount of its secretion on the surface of the ground. Wherever a deer travels, it leaves a "scented trail" on the ground. Any other deer traveling through this same area later on recognizes this "scented trail" as that of another deer's safe route of travel and naturally follows. This is basically how deer develop the trail systems within their herd's home range territory, by leaving interdigital scent on the ground for other members of the herd to follow. Deer are herd animals, and by being so, they are naturally very social. They seek out and follow other deer for companionship and safety, just as cows and other herd animals do. How close in distance one deer will allow another deer to follow behind it, or bed or feed near it, varies greatly depending on each deer's age, aggressiveness, dominance ranking, and tolerance.

Another situation showing how deer use interdigital

scent to safely guide their travels would be when a deer running along the edge of a field suddenly turns into the woods. The "scented trail" left on the ground earlier by another deer, as it entered the woods from the field at that location, indicates a safe route for other deer to follow.

The metatarsal glands are located on the outside of the deer's lower, hind legs, just above what most people would refer to as the deer's ankle. The function of the deer's metatarsal glands is to warn other deer of danger. When a deer is suddenly alarmed, then spooks and runs, the metatarsal glands, triggered by the deer's excited state of mind, automatically flare open and release a small puff of scent that settles on the ground and on any low vegetation it may contact. This lingering odor serves to warn any other deer in the immediate area, or those that follow later on, that something is wrong here. Should another deer happen to walk into this "scented area" ten to thirty minutes later, it would be instantly alerted to the "danger signal," and leave that area without any hesitation whatsoever. Furthermore, it may also spray the area with its own metatarsal scent, to further warn other deer that may follow this same "scented trail" later on and so on. This is why you should never walk directly on, or too close to any deer trails. They will definitely pick up your scent on the ground, and know you have been there. Believe it!

From the first days of their lives fawns follow their parental doe everywhere she goes. This behavioral condition naturally teaches the young fawns to follow the interdigital scent left on the ground by their mother. As fawns follow their mother's "scented trail" they also instinctively learn to associate danger and run whenever their parental doe sprays her metatarsal scent and runs away. After fawns have been rejected from their family group and they are out on their own, they follow and use the "scented trails" of other deer within their herd to safely guide their daily travels. This is how nature instills the behavioral trait for a deer to follow other deer. It has been going on since the beginning of time, and it will never change!

The tarsal glands, also called the *musk glands*, are located on the inside of the deer's hind legs, at what most people commonly call the deer's knee joint. The tarsal glands are the source of a deer's personal identity. All deer have different, individual "musk odors" that deer use to identify one deer from another.

Deer develop trails and establish their home range areas by depositing interdigital scent on the ground wherever they travel, and by urinating on their tarsal glands and marking the ground with their own, personal "musk scent." These marking spots are called *scrapes*. All deer, young and old, make scrapes to scent and mark their home range areas. When deer make ground scrapes and mark their home range areas with their urine in combination with their own, personal "musk odor," other deer recognize that a certain individual deer or a certain family group of deer live in that area.

One of the first things a deer does when it has been trapped and released into a new area, or when a fawn or yearling deer is first rejected from its family group, is to urinate on its tarsal glands and mark the ground with its own, personal "musk scent." From that starting point, it begins to develop its new home range area. This is why you find many scrapes in the woods during late spring, summer, and early fall, just before the *rut* begins. Young deer are establishing their own home range areas. Mature bucks make scrapes and mark their home range areas more extensively than normal just before and during the rut, and I will explain this marking activity in much greater detail later on in the book. I do not want to confuse your mind with any more information about scrapes other than what you need to know right now.

Deer do not always travel directly on well-established herd trails. They frequently walk and browse downwind of a herd's main trail, and use the interdigital scent of other deer already deposited on the trails to guide their movement while feeding or traveling. Main herd trails are used more by the deer of the herd during periods of heavy hunting pressure, winter storms, etc. Many of the deer herd trail systems and home range territories used by the deer that you are hunting today have probably existed for many years, and may have been used by many generations of deer in the past. Some deer trail systems have existed for hundreds of years. I have seen deer trails in the mountains that deer have been using for so long that their hooves have actually worn deep grooves into the solid rock. Deer trail systems do not change unless the land, or the land use, changes. The winds and other climatic conditions control which trails the deer use.

Deer have three basic gaits of movement they use to travel: walking, trotting, and running, with variations of slow to fast within each gait. Under natural conditions deer usually walk everywhere they go. Deer trot when they are alarmed, and they run when they are spooked.

When deer walk, they naturally travel with their head and nose twelve to eighteen inches off the ground. Nature designed this head-down walking posture so that deer are able to effortlessly scent the ground or the trails they walk on without lifting and lowering their heads, wasting energy every time they need to check the scent on the ground or the wind to their back.

Deer usually never run unless they are spooked. When a deer or a group of deer run through the woods, something has definitely spooked them. Deer never run just for the

Tarsal glands, also called "musk glands," are located on the inside of the deer's hind legs at what is commonly called the knee joint.

hell of it. When a deer runs, it burns off two to three times the amount of calories it normally uses when walking. Deer—like any animal in nature—expend no more energy than absolutely necessary. This is one of nature's laws of survival!

A deer running means danger to other deer. A deer running anywhere in the deer herd's home range territory alerts the entire herd to approaching danger. Young deer run around in play to develop their leg muscles and their agility, but these activities usually stop as they mature. Bucks trot and run around chasing does during the rut, as part of the courtship and mating ritual, to separate a particular doe from other deer. This is normal deer behavior under these conditions, but it is not considered normal behavior under normal conditions. If you ever have the occasion to watch the other deer of the herd when young deer run around wildly in play, or when a buck chases a doe around during the rut, most times you will see that the other deer usually become very nervous and fidgety, and, many times, they run away from the area, or after a few tense seconds, most of the deer settle down and return to their normal activity.

It is pretty obvious that whitetail deer are called so because of their white hindparts and tail. There is a definite purpose in nature for the white coloration of a deer's rump area. It is a part of the deer herd's defense system. When a deer is suddenly spooked and it runs away, all a predator really sees is flashes of white spots, bouncing up and down, going off through the woods in all different directions. The purpose of this behavior and flashy display is to startle and briefly confuse a predator for a few split seconds of precious time, which deer use to put some distance between them and danger. The deer runs off in leaps and bounds, but usually only for short distances. Then they drop their tails back down and the bouncing, flashy white spots disappear. This serves to further confuse the predator into thinking that the deer has disappeared in flight, because it has lost sight of the bouncing, white flashes. In reality, the deer have just stopped to watch and wait, to see if anything follows them. When deer raise their tails and expose their white rump patches, it also tends to mentally de-

Whitetails flag, or raise their tails, whenever alarmed or when they spook and run. The flag serves as a visual warning to other deer.

feat the predator by showing that the deer are aware of its presence, and that any chance of a surprise attack, or of stalking in closer without the deer seeing them, is lost.

Deer raise their tails or flag whenever they become alarmed or spook and run. It is a nervous reaction, and a "warning signal" to other deer. Any deer following near or behind another deer when it flags knows that something is wrong, and it will usually freeze in its place until the alarmed deer either settles down and moves on or spooks and runs.

Whitetail deer also use a few vocal sounds to communi-

Whitetail does are capable of up to five estrous or heat cycles per year. This mature whitetail buck in hard antler passes by a very young spotted fawn—think about the timing required for this to occur!

cate with each other. Most of these vocal sounds are soft "bleats" and "baahs" that parental does use to call or discipline their fawns. Fawns also use "bleats" and "baahs" to get their mother's attention.

Whitetail deer also make very loud, long, ear-shattering "blaaaahs" when they have been severely injured or immobilized and frightened. This is another "danger warning signal" that immediately alarms and spooks other deer.

Whitetail deer also use another very distinctive, vocal

"danger warning signal" when they become alarmed or spooked. It is called a *blow*, and it is a loud, whistle-type of noise that is caused by bursts of air being quickly expelled through the deer's nostrils. Blows, also called *snorts*, are very loud and they carry for great distances. Any deer within hearing distance of a blow knows danger is near. All whitetail deer, young and old, are capable of sounding a blow to warn other deer of danger. Generally, the louder, deeper sounding blows are made by the larger deer, but there is really no way to tell if the blow was made by a large doe or a buck, as they both sound the same.

Deer usually blow warnings to other deer when they instantly recognize the sight, sound, or scent of danger—such as a human hunter walking along the edge of a field before daylight, or the strong, stinky scent of a human sleeping beside a tree in the woods, etc. Many times a deer will blow and alternately stamp their front feet to the ground, then spray its metatarsal scent after detecting the scent of danger close by on the ground or in the air. Other times, the deer will blow constantly, in two to three second intervals, as it slowly walks or trots away from an area. It all depends on each deer's previous life experiences, and its state of mind. If a deer ever blows at you while you are hunting in a ground blind or up in a treestand, immediately move yourself far away from that area, or your hunt could be over for the day.

Whitetail does are capable of having up to five estrous or heat cycles per year, all depending on the age of the doe, the population of their herd, the availability of food, and the number of bucks available to do the mating. Three heat cycles per year is considered normal.

As I mentioned before, daylight is the key to deer life, as it is for just about everything else on this earth. The steadily increasing length of daylight hours during the days of spring and summer is what controls when buds and leaves grow on trees, when flowers bloom, when fruits and nuts begin to grow, etc. The shortening of daylight hours in late summer and early fall controls when the fruits and nuts of plants and trees ripen, when the leaves turn brilliant colors, etc., and it also controls when the does begin their first heat cycle.

The shortening of daylight hours, seen through the doe's eyes over a period of time, causes the pituitary glands, the deer's "biological clock," to increase the hormone levels in their body to a certain trigger point. This, combined with the rising full moon, causes estrous to occur. All does do not begin their estrous cycle at the exact, same time. It is an individual, random occurrence that is all controlled by each doe's biological age, nutritional state, and physical health. However, most all does will begin their heat cycles within seven days, before or after the full moon. Most women experience their menstrual cycle during this same time frame.

The doe's first estrous cycle begins to occur with the rising full moon, near the early part of October in the section of the country where I live and generally hunt. Whitetail does living in the more northern latitudes of the United States will begin to experience their first heat cycle with the rising full moon near the early part of September, and does living in the more southern latitudes will begin their first estrous cycle with the rising full moon near the early part of November.

The doe's first estrous cycle is considered to be a *false heat* because it generally only lasts for three to five hours. Normally does will not accept bucks for mating during their first heat cycle because they are just not biologically ready yet. This first, very short heat cycle functions more

A young buck repeatedly trying to mount its parental doe in early October is a clear sign that the doe's first estrous cycle has begun.

as a timing device for nature. It sets up the deer's main breeding season or rut to occur twenty-six to twenty-eight days later, during the doe's second heat cycle, near the full moon in early to mid-November. It also establishes that the birthing season of fawns, approximately 200 days after mating, occurs in the spring of the year, when the weather is mild and food is plentiful.

Once a doe experiences her first heat cycle, she will cycle back into estrous every twenty-six to twenty-eight days, for twenty-four to thirty-six hours, until she becomes pregnant. Generally, most does are bred during their second heat cycle. Any does that were not successfully mated during the main rut experience their third heat cycle twenty-six to twenty-eightdays later, near the full moon in early to mid-December, and so on, through January and February. If you hunt in the extreme northern or southern latitudes of the United States, just use the timing of the doe's first heat cycle in your area to determine the occurrence of the main rut and the doe's remaining estrous cycles. If you are not sure of when the doe's first heat cycle occurs in your area, just watch the leaves on the trees. When the leaves first begin to change to their fall colors, near a rising full moon, the does living in your area will begin to experience their first estrous cycle.

If you see a male fawn or yearling repeatedly trying to mount its parental doe, or see it constantly nosing her vulva during early October, you can safely assume the doe is probably in her first heat cycle. Remember the date, the weather conditions, and the direction of the wind, because twenty-six to twenty-eight days after that date, you should be hunting in that doe's home range area. The doe will be in estrous and any bucks in the area will be after her.

In bucks, the slowly increasing levels of daylight conditions in the late spring and early summer stimulate their pituitary glands to increase the levels of male hormones or testosterone in their bodies to a certain trigger point that causes their antlers to begin growing. The rate of antler growth, and the size of each buck's set of antlers, is determined by age, genetics, and nutrition. Most Whitetail bucks grow a symmetrical or typical set of antlers. Most of the non-symmetrical or non-typical antler formations found on many Whitetail bucks are the result of injuries directly to their antlers while they were in their growing stage. Many antler injuries are caused as a result of being jumped from their beds by dogs or other predators, with the buck running through thick greenbrier, honeysuckle, young pine trees, etc., to escape and catching or banging the tender, growing antlers on vines, brush, small tree limbs, etc. Some non-typical antler formations are the direct result of severe body injuries incurred during the previous year, which normally affects the side opposite the body injury. As daylight conditions slowly fall to certain critical levels that bring on the does' first heat cycle in the early fall, testosterone in the bucks rises to near peak levels, which causes them to become very aggressive and solitary.

Throughout the late spring and summer months, the bucks of the herd often travel and feed with each other. Their dominance over the family groups of the herd determines where they bed and when they move out to feed. Since most of the bucks normally bed down somewhere behind the family groups, and they all usually leave their beds at about the same time of day, the bucks of the herd are always aware of each other's presence. Deer, including the bucks, are herd animals and very social, and since their survival depends on "safety in numbers," the bucks naturally seek out other bucks for companionship.

CHAPTER FOUR

RUBS, SCRAPES, AND TRAILS

Young bucks learn most of their adult behavior while traveling with or being near an older buck when something strange occurs, just as they learned things when they were fawns traveling with their parental doe. Young deer survive by learning the life experiences of other deer. They never forget what they have learned, and they never even have to think about it again. It becomes a conditioned, behavioral response!

If a young buck observes an older, wiser buck reacting to a certain situation, the young buck is taught, right then, to react to the same situation the same way the older buck did. Should that young buck ever experience that same situation in the future, it will instinctively, automatically react as it was taught to do. It is much like the way young boys learn things from their fathers by mere association. The young bucks see how the older bucks react to different situations, and their behavior automatically shifts to whatever the older, wiser bucks did. If an older buck spooked and ran away whenever a certain scent or sound was detected in the air, let's say, the scent of a human wearing "fox scent," or the sound of a loud truck muffler pounding through the forest, or a human blowing some kind of deer call, the young buck, seeing the older buck spook and run as it detected this same strange odor or sound in the air, is instantly taught to quickly run away whenever that scent or sound appears ever again.

Nature changes this close association of the herd's bucks and their traveling around together in spring and summer by increasing the testosterone levels in their bodies to certain other trigger points, which in turn affects and alters their normal biological and social behavior. As testosterone levels in the buck slowly rise to a certain critical point, the flow of blood feeding the antlers is shut off. This stops antler growth and causes the antlers to air dry or cure, and harden over a short period of time. Once the antlers harden the dried out, outer covering, called *velvet*, slowly splits apart, and many times hangs down off the buck's antlers in ragged, dangling pieces. This becomes bothersome to the buck's balance, feel, and sight. So, the bucks rub their antlers up against bushes and small trees to remove the hanging, shaggy, dried pieces of velvet. This pushing and rubbing against bushes and small trees, over a period of time, also serves to smooth and polish the antlers, and it also helps build and strengthen the buck's neck and leg muscles. Once again, this is all controlled by the shortening of daylight hours and this is why bucks rub small trees and bushes at this time of the year.

The bucks of the herd also begin sparring with each other at this time of the year. The still-rising levels of testosterone in their bodies make them very aggressive and less tolerant of each other. They have a lot of nervous energy to burn, so they push and pull against each other in play, which also further helps to develop and strengthen their leg and neck muscles. When the bucks of the herd spar with each other they each display their size and strength against one another. This early sparring activity physically decides the "pecking order position" of each buck in the herd, and determines which bucks are primar-

The development of antlers, shedding of the velvet, and ultimately shedding of the antlers is largely controlled by the levels of testosterone in the buck's body.

ily going to do the mating. The most dominant bucks of the herd do most of the breeding. This early sparring activity also serves to help save the large, mature bucks of the herd from wasting a lot of precious energy in brutal combat with other bucks of the herd later on during the rut, when they will need all their reserve energy to defend their breeding territories, to chase out and mate with does, and to survive.

Once the does begin to experience their first heat cycle, the mature bucks of the herd begin extensively marking out their home range areas during their daily travels within the herd's home range territory. They rub and scent trees, called *rubs*, and make scented ground *scrapes* all around the outermost boundaries of their home range areas. These particular rubs and scrapes are a mature buck's territorial boundary markers. The exact path the mature buck walked when he placed his territorial markers becomes his *territorial trail.* A mature buck's territorial trail is defined and controlled daily by the direction of the wind. As the wind direction changes and the entire herd shifts its travels over to other trails in other areas of the herd's home range territory, the mature bucks rub and scent trees, and make scented ground scrapes in other areas of their home range areas, in other areas of the herd's home range territory.

Territorial rubs and scrapes function like "No Trespassing" signs in the deer's world. The rubbed and scented trees and scented ground scrapes leave a visual and a scented warning to the other bucks of the herd, showing them that the area is claimed and defended by a certain mature buck of the herd. Since it is quite impossible for a mature buck to be everywhere at once to defend his marked out, claimed area in the herd's home range territory, the rubs and scrapes are primarily made to warn other bucks of the herd to stay out of his area when he is not around. If the younger bucks of the herd smell the scent of a big, aggressive herd buck in an area, they tend to stay away from that area. The larger buck's size, strength, and physical dominance over them in the past virtually scares them away—at least until any one of the smaller, herd bucks grows large enough and strong enough to challenge him for his breeding rights and his home range area. The young and the other less dominant, slightly older bucks of the herd still rub a few trees and make a few scented ground scrapes, but they are only mimicking and learning from the older, more dominant bucks of the herd that set up and defend breeding territories. The dominant bucks do most of the mating, and they try to keep the younger

Territorial rubs and scrapes function like "no trespassing" signs in the deer's world, warning other bucks to stay clear of the area.

bucks of the herd away by leaving their scent all over their home range areas.

When a buck makes a ground scrape, he paws the ground with one or both of his front feet alternately to remove leaves, grass, etc., exposing a small area of bare ground approximately twelve to fourteen inches in diameter. Then the buck arches his back and sort of squats so

Whitetail bucks use territorial rubs to help guide their travels along their very seldom used territorial trails during hours of darkness.

that when he urinates, the urine flows out of his penis, down onto his tarsal or musk glands while he is rubbing them against each other. The "musk scented" urine then drips down his rear, lower legs and feet onto the ground, in the bare area of ground that the buck has just cleared. By doing this the buck deposits his own, personal "musk scent" and urine directly in the scrape which soaks into the ground for a lasting effect.

Many times a mature buck will locate a territorial scrape beside a small tree that has a few head-high branches that tend to hang out over the scrape, near where his territorial trail crosses a well-established herd trail. The buck will usually lick his musk glands with his tongue, then mouth or lick some of the branches directly above the scrape to put more of his personal "musk scent" around the area of the scrape. Sometimes a buck will even stand up on a his hind legs and mouth and lick the branches a little higher up in the tree to get his "musk scent" up higher in the air, to further intimidate the younger bucks by making them believe that he is much bigger than he actually is. Any other herd bucks or deer that travel within scenting distance of these territorial markers are instantly aware of the mature buck's presence by his strong, musky odor left in and around the scrape. Unless any other herd bucks feel like they want to challenge his strength and his dominant position in the herd, they will usually avoid his claimed territory.

Mature herd bucks usually make ground scrapes wherever a herd doe's trail crosses their territorial trail. If you ever find five or six small scrapes real close together, all within five to twelve yards of each other along the same trail, a mature buck's territorial trail probably crossed the "scented trails" left by five to six herd does that walked through that same area a short distance apart from each other. And the buck marked each one of those crossing spots with his personal "musk scent" to attract the doe's attention whenever they travel on those trails again, for mating purposes later on. This is why whitetail bucks make a lot of ground scrapes at this time of year. They mark their territorial boundaries with them to warn other deer that they are entering a claimed area, and they use them to attract the does for mating.

A mature buck will usually locate his territorial rubs within an eyesight's distance from one to another as he travels along his territorial trail. Bucks use these rubbed trees during the hours of darkness and other low, light conditions to help guide them around on their very seldom traveled territorial trails. Bucks only travel on their territorial trails when they need to freshen the scent on their territorial rubs and scrapes. Since the bucks do not travel on their territorial trails very often they do not leave enough interdigital scent on the ground to show them where they traveled when they first marked out their territorial boundaries. The bare, light, colored areas on the rubbed trees brightly shine out to the buck's eyes in the dark of night, when he is normally the most active. The rubs guide his travels to help him locate the territorial scrapes he previously made along the same territorial trail—especially right after a rain or snowstorm ends, when his scent on them has been totally washed away.

When a buck makes a tree rub, he usually faces the tree and rubs the tree with the rough areas of his main beams, near the brown tines, in a low, head-down position. The rough areas found on the main beams of a buck's antlers are the dried up passages of blood vessels that supplied the antlers with blood during their growing period. Most bucks are unable to completely smooth out these areas when they rub on trees and bushes to remove the velvet and polish their antlers, because these areas are just too close to the buck's eyes. The buck pushes against the tree and, at the same time, alternately rubs the main beams on each side of his antlers up and down, pushing back and forth against the tree until the bark is removed from a small area of the tree. Then the buck usually licks his musk

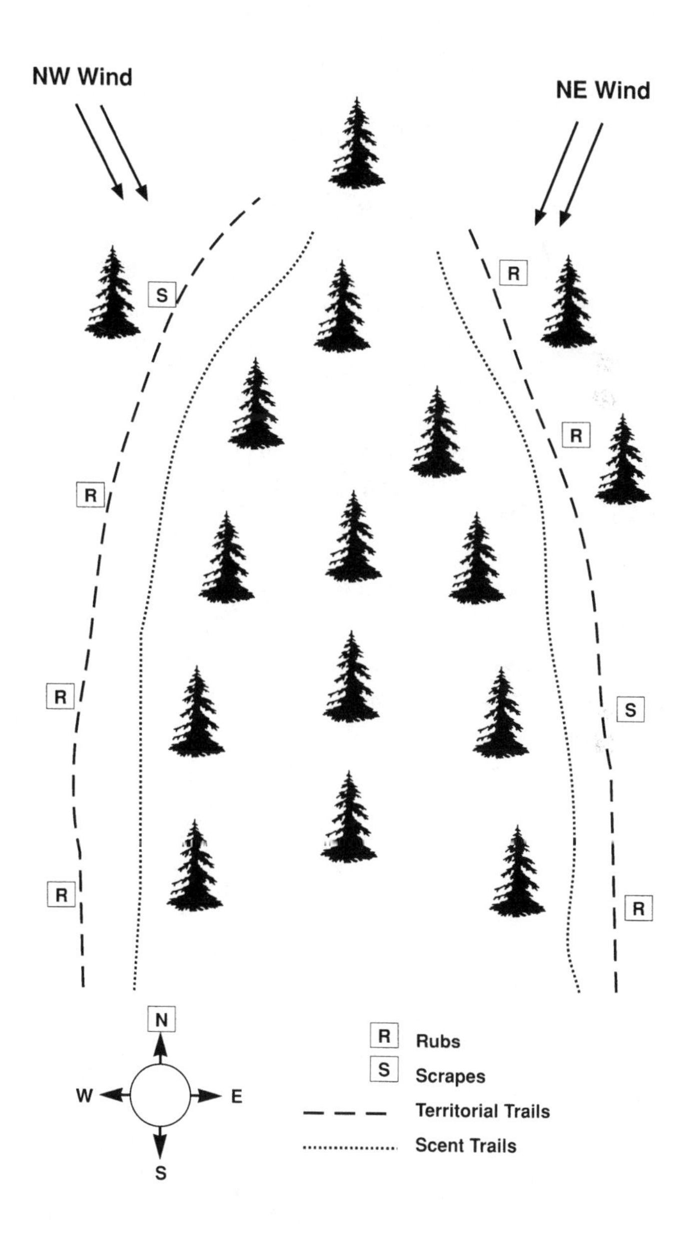
NW Wind
NE Wind
S
R
R
R
R
R
R
S
R
N
W
E
S
R Rubs
S Scrapes
Territorial Trails
Scent Trails

glands, and then licks the exposed, bare area of the tree that he has rubbed clear. By doing so, the buck puts his personal "musk scent" directly on the rubbed tree, so that other deer are made aware of his scent and his territorial marker. A buck does not necessarily need to lick his tarsal glands every time he makes a tree rub, because generally enough tarsal scent is transferred to the buck's tongue, lips, and muzzle area during the gland-licking process to scent many territorial markers. The buck usually only licks his tarsal glands when he needs more "musk scent" to mark other territorial rubs.

A few years ago some overzealous outdoor writers published some incorrect information in articles and books that stated that "bucks rub their 'preorbital glands' on overhanging branches above their scrapes for scenting purposes." Well, they were very wrong!

The preorbital glands on deer, located near the corner of each eye, are "tear ducts," and they do not produce any identifying body scent at all. Their function is to produce a natural cleansing solution that cleans the deer's eyes and keeps them moist. That is their purpose, and nothing else! Whitetail deer may occasionally rub the areas of their preorbital glands against small tree branches, on their front legs, or on anything else that will help remove the congealed, crusted, or gooey residue from the deer's eyelid areas for better vision, just as dogs, horses, and other animals on this earth do.

Recently, a few equally overzealous outdoor writers discovered a research article about "Forehead Glands in Whitetail Deer" and they, all by themselves, determined that the pelage or hair covering in the forehead area of male deer functions as a scent-producing gland. And they published that whitetail bucks rub their foreheads on the trees

Bucks use scent trails to scent-check the condition of their rubs and scrapes. Left, a well-traveled scent trail splits off from a seldom-traveled territorial trail—which actually holds the rubs and scrapes.

that they rub with their antlers, which supposedly leaves their scent on these rubbed trees.

As usual, these writers jumped the gun again and published "their ideas" to the deer hunting world on this matter. They used the partial, unconfirmed, and unproven research of others to sell their stories of "how bucks scent their rubs." This is much like the "bucks rub their preorbital glands on branches to scent their scrapes" situation that I described to you earlier. Once again, it is a simple case of the wrong information, in the wrong hands!

What the study did not show was that the forehead areas on both bucks and does, young and old, showed seasonal changes in the forehead pelage or hair covering that was consistent with the rest of the deer's seasonal coat.

What these writers failed to point out in their published articles was that many other animals on this earth, especially the males of many species, usually undergo various biological and physiological changes which make them appear more aggressive looking to other males of their species and more attractive to the females as breeding partners. And, that the skin tissue underlying the forehead areas of many of the antlered and horned males of many different species physiologically changes during their mating seasons to also help withstand the impact of heads, antlers, and horns during dominance sparring or head-to-head combat for the breeding rights of the females of their species.

As a professional taxidermist and operator of a successful taxidermy studio for many years, I have personally skinned out and examined over 1,500 deer heads, and I have never seen or found any type of glandular duct system in or underneath the skin of the forehead areas of any of these deer, which are obvious in the other scent producing glands found on other areas of the deer's body. Furthermore, when a buck rubs a tree with his antlers, the angle of his antlers in relationsip to his forehead while he is rubbing the tree almost physically prevents the buck's forehead and muzzle from ever touching the tree. And, I have never seen two whitetail bucks, or any other whitetail deer, greet each other by sniffing at their forehead areas. And, in other recent scientific studies that were not generally reported to the hunting public, tracking dogs were unable to detect any noticeable scent from the forehead areas of whitetail deer, male or female, unlike other known species of the deer family that do have scent producing glandular duct systems located in their forehead areas!

It is "wrong information" such as this that is published in national magazines that continues to confuse deer hunters about the deer's natural behavior. It would seem that some of these outdoor writers should spend more of their time in the woods watching and studying the natural behavior of deer and writing about what they actually see, rather than

Although the relationship is not exact, large bucks tend to rub large territorial trees.

just reading and publishing the incomplete, unproven hypotheses of others that are commonly published in many scientific journals.

Once a mature buck marks out a territorial trail with territorial rubs and scrapes, he usually will not travel on that territorial trail again for several days, or until right after it rains or snows. His very strong "musk scent" deposited on rubbed trees and in the ground scrapes normally lasts for many days, and he will only travel on that trail again when he needs to refresh them. If a buck marks a section of his territorial trail when the wind is out of the northwest, you will only see him traveling on that same section of the territorial trail when the wind is out of the northwest again, and that is only if those rubs and scrapes need to be freshened.

A mature buck normally uses a *scent trail* to check the

condition of the rubs and scrapes on his territorial trail. A buck's scent trail runs somewhat parallel to his territorial trail, and it is usually located twenty to eighty yards on the downwind side of his territorial trail, depending on the terrain. A mature buck travels his scent trail regularly when the direction of the wind is right for him to be traveling through the area, to scent-check the conditions of his rubs and scrapes. When a buck travels on his scent trail and passes by each one of the territorial markers on his territorial trail at some distance downwind and slightly parallel, the buck merely tosses his nose into the wind that is coming off his back from the direction of the rub or scrape that he has just passed and scent-checks the strength of his "musk scent" on the rub or scrape. A buck will not normally waste the time and energy it takes to physically walk up to, and check, each territorial marker. However, a buck will go to any one of his territorial markers that need to be freshened and he can tell which ones from downwind on his scent trail.

Mature bucks usually locate their territorial rubs and scrapes along the high ground areas of land that surround the low, bottomland areas of the herd's home range territory. Since mature bucks are normally the most active during the night, while the nighttime cool air thermals are falling down into all the low areas of the land, the buck can easily scent-check the condition of many of his high ground rubs and scrapes by simply traveling through the bottomlands on his scent trail with the thermal or wind to his back. Once again, this serves to save the buck time and energy.

If you hunt of a mature buck near any one of his scented high ground rubs or scrapes in early morning or late afternoon, the buck will probably scent you from downwind and know that you are there, and learn you scent. I don't believe you should ever put anything into a mature buck's scrape, or he will know about it and he will probably change his scent trail through the area or avoid that scrape and that entire area altogether. You should hunt for him somewhere along his scent trail, where he travels the most.

If you find a mature buck's territorial rubs and scrapes, the side of the tree that is rubbed clean, and the direction of his tracks found in his scrapes will show you the direction he was moving when he made his territorial markers. With just those signs alone, you can pretty much determine what the direction of the wind was on the day he made them.

If you happen to find a lot of rubbed trees in a particular area it usually means that at least two mature bucks have territorial trails and home range areas that are very close to each other. In this situation, each buck will usually rub and scent a few extra territorial boundary trees to warn the other buck to stay out of his territory. This is a real good area to hunt right after a rain- or snowstorm ends. Each buck, sooner or later when the wind direction is right for him to be traveling through that area again, will be back there to freshen their "musk scent" on their territorial rubs. Rain and snow wash away the buck's scent from his rubs and scrapes, and the first thing most every mature whitetail buck does right after the rain or snow stops, is to freshen the scent of their territorial rubs and scrapes with their "musk scent" and reclaim their mating territory.

All bucks occasionally rub small trees, but big, mature bucks rub big territorial trees. Unless the terrain changes or the mature buck dies, he will usually rub the same territorial trees year after year until the tree dies. Then the buck will usually locate a new territorial rub somewhere near the old marker. Many of the territorial trees rubbed by very

Scrapes are cleared and freshened soon after rain- and windstorms end—provided the wind conditions are right for the bucks to travel in those areas again.

large, mature bucks are sometimes six to eight inches in diameter. Generally, the larger the tree, the larger the buck.

Many times the strong windstorms that usually occur in October and November blow a lot of leaves off the trees which fall to the ground and sometimes cover up a buck's scrapes. Bucks will usually clear off and freshen their scrapes right after the winds die down, when the wind direction is right for the buck to travel on that section of his territorial trail again. These are about the only times that you want to be hunting anywhere near a buck's territorial rubs and scrapes. Otherwise, you are just wasting your very limited time, hunting near the territorial markers of a buck that probably will not visit there again for a long time. Once again, territorial rubs and scrapes function like "No Trespassing Signs" for mature bucks when they are not around. Their "musk and urine" scent alone serves to warn other bucks of the herd to stay away. Mature bucks do not return to their territorial scrapes and rub unless they need to be freshened, and you should always hunt for the buck somewhere along his scent trail, unless you are hunting right after the rain or snow ends!

I took one of my finest trophy whitetail bucks hunting twenty yards downwind of his scent trail. I was bow hunting in early October, just before the full moon, and I knew that some of the does in the area were beginning to experience their first estrous cycle. I had seen a male yearling trying to mount its parental doe in the woods two days prior. I had located this particular buck's territorial trail and scent trail during the late winter of the previous year while I was out looking for shed antlers. So, I had a pretty good idea of where I wanted to start hunting for them. But, you never know, he could have been hit by a car, or died of old age or something else during the past spring or summer.

CHAPTER FIVE

THE ESTROUS CYCLE AND MASTER SCRAPES

I set up my portable treestand in the morning darkness and waited for daylight to break. I wanted to watch a particular area of the woods and a section of the buck's old scent trail just to see what was happening here in the early morning hours. The sky was partly cloudy; the wind was mild and out of the east. According to the sides of the rubbed trees and the tracks that I found the past winter, this particular buck was traveling through this area during easterly winds. If he was still alive, I figured this buck would move through this area again whenever the winds were out of the east.

About an hour after daylight my eyes caught something moving through a low brush area of open woods, fifty to sixty yards upwind of me. It appeared to be the same buck that had made the rubs the previous year. He was walking slow, with his head down in a normal, natural, walking position on the same scent trail that I had found the past winter. I timed his appearance at 7:18 a.m. After the buck disappeared from my sight, I went over to where he had just walked through to compare his tracks with other tracks that I had found during late winter. I also noticed that he had just recently rubbed one of the same trees that he used last year as one of his territorial markers. My first thoughts were that I was going to come back to this area again when the weather conditions were similar and the winds out of the east.

That night I watched the nightly weather report for the next day's weather conditions. It called for partly cloudy skies and the winds to be out of the east—the same exact conditions under which I saw the big buck moving naturally through the woods while I was hunting. It was time to hunt that area again!

I returned to the same section of woods that I was hunting the day before, except this time I set up my portable treestand on a tree twenty to twenty-five yards downwind of the buck's scent trail, near where he walked the morning before and waited for him to show. At 7:20 a.m. I saw him coming toward me on his scent trail, and when the buck passed by me, fully broadside, I released an arrow through both his lungs. This fine buck dressed out at 204 pounds and carried a massive, 10-point rack that scored 159 3/8 P&Y. This was all made possible by understanding how mature bucks use their scent trails and the wind.

Once the doe's first estrous cycle occurs, the mature bucks become very anxious, like nervous boxers loosening up before a big fight. They want to breed, but the does are just not biologically ready to mate yet. The bucks are frustrated and they have a lot of nervous energy to burn. They are biologically driven to move around a lot more now, because of the high level of testosterone in their bodies. So, the bucks tend to follow closer behind the does of the herd, many times traveling right with them, waiting for any one of the does to begin their second heat cycle. Bucks seek out the does, and if you know where the does of the herd feed and bed under all different weather conditions and wind directions, you will have a pretty good chance of seeing a large, mature buck traveling with them at this time of the year, since the does normally travel around during

This big ten-point, field-dressing at 204 pounds and scoring 159 3/8 P&Y, was taken from a position twenty yards downwind of his scent trail.

the low daylight conditions of early morning and late afternoon and the bucks are starting to follow the does around. The bucks will be traveling around more in daylight and that makes them very vulnerable. This is about the only time of the year, during the mating season, that you will ever see a mature whitetail buck traveling around in daylight under natural conditions.

When any one of the does in the herd begins to experience their second heat cycle in early November, the primary rut begins. Once again, this is all controlled by the shortening of daylight hours and the rising full moon. Some hunters falsely believe that the colder air temperatures and early morning frosts at this time of the year are somehow responsible for when the does' estrous cycles occur. This is totally false and unfounded. If cold temperatures controlled when whitetail deer mate, most deer living in the South or the southeastern United States would never breed.

When a doe begins her estrous cycle her vulva swells and becomes very moist with vaginal secretions. The doe's vaginal secretions slowly seep out of her vulva and drip down the back of her hind legs. The movement of her rear legs and her rear hooves striking the ground as she travels jars or shakes small drops of this secretion off her legs and vulva onto the ground and this creates a heavily scented *sex trail* on the ground wherever she goes. As the doe travels to and from various bedding and feeding areas, controlled by the direction of the wind, the doe leaves a very strong sex trail on the ground for a buck to find and follow.

When sexually mature bucks scent the sex trail of a doe in estrous on the ground or in the wind, or sniffs at their vulva area, the buck usually displays a somewhat contorted, upper lip curl called a "Flehman posture." This is a biophysical reaction to the sexual, chemical attractant of female animals in estrous, called pheromones. This is normal behavior for all sexually mature bucks during the rut.

Most times an older, more mature doe in heat will urinate on its musk glands while it is standing over a mature buck's scrape, when it is ready to mate. By doing so, the doe deposits her own, personal "musk scent," along with urine and vaginal secretions, directly in the buck's scrape. These older does are eager to mate and bear fawns. This is their purpose in nature. They have learned from their past mating experiences and by watching the other does of the herd over past mating seasons how to best attract a breeding buck quickly to them to mate while they are in estrous.

You can easily tell when the does are in their second heat cycle. Their musk glands change from a tan or light brown color to a blackish, dark color. Their urine and vaginal secretions, combined with their musk gland secretions, alter or stain their color when they urinate on them and rub them together. The musk glands change to this blackish

Large, mature bucks like this do not normally travel around in daylight under natural conditions—except during the rut.

color each time the does cycle into heat, and the musk glands remain this dark color until the does go out of estrous. You can easily see the blackened musk glands on their rear legs when they walk at a fair distance away. They really do stand out!

After an older doe urinates on her musk glands, on the mature buck's scrape, she will usually only travel a short distance away from the scrape, bed down, and wait for the buck to find her or her sex trail. When the mature buck travels through this same section of the herd's home range territory, controlled by the same wind conditions that guided the doe into this area, and the buck finds the doe's sex trail crossing his territorial trail or scrape, the buck follows her scented sex trail until he finds her. Once the buck locates the doe that is in estrous, he stays right with the doe wherever she goes to keep other bucks of the herd away from her, and he frequently mates with her until she goes out of heat. Then the mature buck usually returns to his marked out home range area in the herd's home range territory, and continues scent-checking his rubs and scrapes on his scent trail, waiting for another herd doe in estrous to travel into his area. This is basically how all mature bucks set up and use their marked, territorial breeding areas during the early stages of rut. As more does of the herd begin to go into heat, the rut gets slightly more complicated.

The wind controls where all the deer of the herd bed, feed, and travel. As long as the wind remains in one basic direction for a period of time, the entire herd lives and stays in the same area of the herd's home range territory until the wind changes direction again. All deer in the herd do not necessarily travel on the same, exact trails, or at the same, exact time. But, over a period of time, usually within three hours, most deer of the herd will usually pass through the same area of the herd's home range territory and the same marked, territorial breeding area of the herd's most dominant buck.

Once a doe begins her estrous cycle and urinates over her musk glands, leaving her scent in one of the mature buck's scrapes, the other deer of the herd that are traveling through this same area are naturally drawn to the area of that particular scrape by the doe's sex trail and her scent left in the scrape. As other does of the herd randomly go into heat and travel through this same area of the herd's home range territory they are drawn to the area of this scented scrape and now their sex trails attract the other bucks of the herd to the scrape.

If the mature, herd buck that claimed this breeding area is currently paired up with a doe that is in estrous and he is not in the area of that scrape to defend it, these other herd bucks, drawn to the area by various does sex trails, each

You can easily tell when a whitetail doe is in estrous; the center of her tarsal or musk glands, visible on the inside of her left rear "knee," turn from tan to a dark, blackened color.

mark the scrape with their own, personal "musk scent," and this one, particular scrape that the herd has been scenting becomes one of the herd's main breeding scrapes, which I call a *master scrape*. As long as the direction of the wind remains constant, it (the wind) controls and directs the entire herd to travel through this section of the herd's home range territory, the mature buck's breeding area, and to this one particular master scrape. As more deer of the herd continue to scent this scrape, they clear more leaves, etc., from the dirt area of the scrape and make it much larger in size. I have seen many master scrapes that were used by a herd of deer so long that the bare ground area of the scrape was cleared four to six feet in diameter by the time the rut ended.

If the wind changes direction, the entire herd's daily travel shifts over to other areas of the herd's home range territory. Other master scrapes are developed in those areas, if the direction of the wind again remains constant for a while. This is one reason why some hunters who are lucky enough to find a master scrape while they are out hunting or scouting on one day see no deer near the area of the master scrape, or notice that the master scrape has not been touched by a deer when they return to hunt near that master scrape a few days or a week later. The wind probably changed direction and the entire herd shifted their daily bedding and feeding activities over to another area of the herd's home range territory, which could be a few miles away from the master scrape that they found. Those hunters, not realizing what has happened, usually spend most of their limited hunting time during the rut hunting near a dead master scrape that will not be active again until the wind shifts back to the direction under which that master scrape was created.

If you find a master scrape, try to determine the direction the deer were traveling when they approached the scrape, and the location of the mature buck's scent trail downwind. You can easily tell if the scrape is currently being used by the amount of leaves, twigs, etc., in the exposed dirt area. Windstorms and shifting winds usually blow all types of debris into the clear, open dirt area of the scrape, and it usually stays there until the mature buck, or other deer of the herd, clear it off.

You can sometimes tell how fresh any scrape is by just sniffing the strength of deer scent left in the scrape. If the scent smells strong and musky to your nose, the deer have probably scented it not too long ago. The direction of deer tracks or the pawing marks of the mature buck's front hooves in the scrape, fresh or old, will show you the direc-

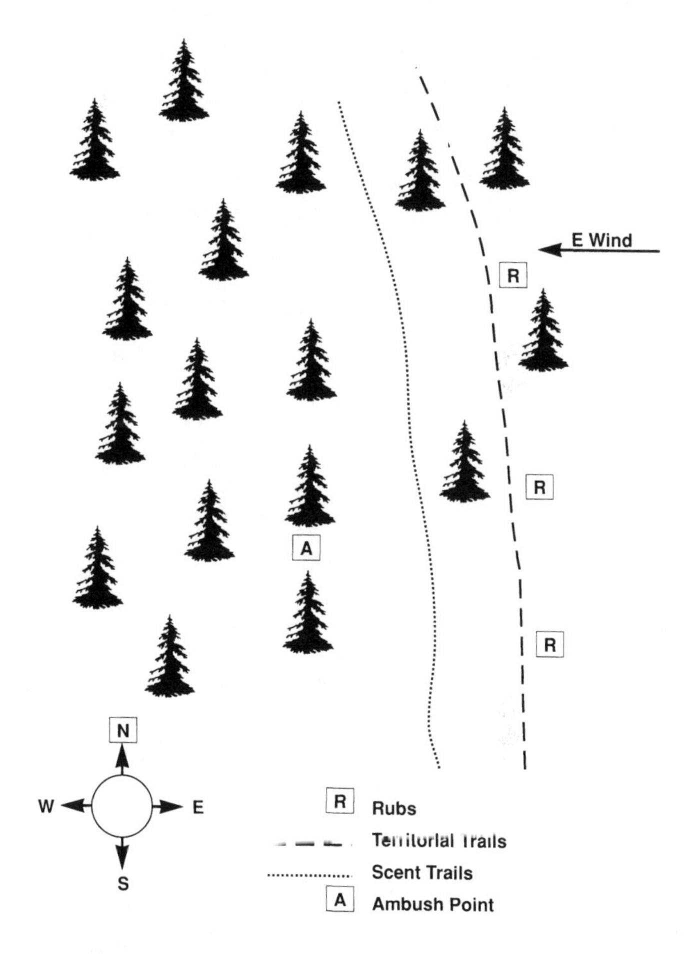

tion that the deer were traveling when they last visited that scrape, and with your compass you can roughly determine what the wind direction was when the deer were there last.

If it has not rained in the area in which you are hunting for a long time and the ground is too dry or too hard to show much deer sign and you cannot find any tracks or paw marks in a scrape to show you the direction the deer

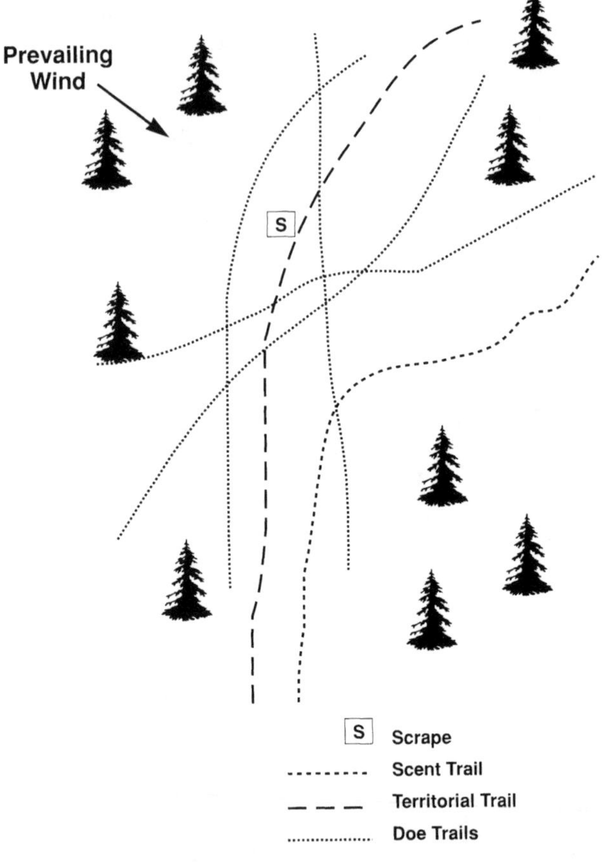

During the *rut,* doe trails will become *sex trails.* A *scrape* near where several *sex trails* occur will probably become a *master scrape.*

are traveling, here is a little trick that I frequently use to determine the direction of deer travel on any trail, and what the wind direction is when the deer use that trail. It is very simple, and it works great! Take a piece of any dark colored thread, two to three feet long. Tie one end of it ten to twelve inches off the ground, around the trunk of a small tree or sapling that is located a foot or so off to one side of the deer trail. Now, tie the other end of the thread to one end of a small, pencil-sized dead branch or stick fourteen to sixteen inches long. Stretch the thread across the deer trail, and push the loose end of the branch into the ground a couple of inches or so, enough to hold the thread stretched tight across the deer trail, eight to ten inches off the ground.

When a deer travels on this trail again, its front legs will strike the thread that is stretched across the trail. The pushing or pulling force on the thread causes the branch to lean in the direction that the deer was traveling. The sapling is rooted in the ground, so it will not move, but the end of the small branch is only stuck in the ground, so it is easily moved when the deer's front legs push on the thread. Sometimes the small branch is pulled completely out of the ground when the deer's front legs strike the thread, but it usually always lies on the ground in the direction the deer was traveling. Either way, the branch shows you the direction that the deer was traveling on the trail, and once you know the direction the deer is traveling, you can use your compass to determine the direction of the wind. You can use this "thread trick" on any deer trail, any time of the year, to show you the direction that deer are traveling on any trail. You do not need to check the thread very often, unless you want to know how often the deer are traveling on that trail, during daylight or darkness, because once it has been tripped by the deer, the small branch remains leaning or lies on the ground in the direction the deer was traveling. All you have to do is check it the next time you are in the area, determine the wind direction, and hunt that area the next time the wind conditions are right.

Once a mature buck pairs up with a doe and leaves the area of his territorial scrape, which is now one of the herd's

"Master scrapes" develop when the direction of the wind remains constant for long periods of time; these scrapes become larger as more bucks in the herd scent and "freshen" them.

master scrapes, the other, less dominant bucks of the herd that are either too old or too young to claim and defend a breeding area usually bed down somewhere near but downwind of the master scrape, and wait for any other does of the herd that are in heat to travel near the scrape. When a larger, more dominant herd buck is paired up with a doe, and he is led off away from the area of the master scrape, all the other less dominant and young bucks of the herd have a chance to breed with any doe that travels near the master scrape. Should a doe in estrous come near the area of the master scrape, these waiting bucks, usually altogether, chase this doe around until the larger, more aggressive buck of the group eventually drives off all the other bucks from the doe and wins her mating rights.

I have seen as many as seven bucks, ranging from spikes to a small eight-pointer, all at the same time chasing a doe in estrous from a master scrape. Once the doe stopped running around and stood for mating, it reminded me of an

African lioness defending her freshly-killed meal from a pack of hungry hyenas. The most dominant buck of the group, a large-bodied six-pointer, finally bred the doe, but only after driving off all the other bucks that were running with the group, one at a time. Each time the six-pointer chased another buck off twenty yards or so, another buck of the group would sneak in and try to mount the doe. When the six-pointer ran that buck off, another buck would try for the doe. This went on for quite a while, with the six- pointer running back and forth, circling around the doe, trying to keep the other bucks away, until he finally had enough time to stop running around to mount her. The other bucks watched it all from nearby. After this mating episode was finished, the six-pointer and the doe traveled off in the distance together, while the other six small bucks all eventually returned back to the area of the master scrape and bedded down, once again, to wait for another doe in heat to come by.

This is one reason why some young bucks are only spike bucks during the second fall of their lives, and why other yearling bucks of the same herd have small, four-point racks on their heads. The parental does of the spike bucks were probably bred by the smaller, younger, less dominant bucks of the herd, and the parental does of the small, four-point yearling bucks were probably bred by the herd's heavier bodied, larger antlered, mature buck. All male fawns enter the first fall of their lives as "button bucks."

Once again, this scrape-watching and mating behavior, witnessed for the first time by some of the younger bucks while they were traveling near or with some of the other, older, less dominant bucks of the herd, is one of the ways that young deer learn about the mating activities of the herd during the rut.

CHAPTER SIX

MOVEMENT IN THE RUT; READING SIGN

When a mature herd buck is paired up with a doe in heat he usually will not return to the area of the master scrape or continue scent-checking any of his territorial rubs and scrapes until that doe goes out of estrous and he wants another doe to mate.

Not all of the does are paired up with bucks because they traveled near a master scrape while they were in heat. Many times, a doe that is in estrous, or its sex trail, is scent-located by the bucks of the herd as the does feed and travel around the herd's home range territory during the night. Most of the courting and mating occurs as the herd travels and feeds during the night, when deer are normally the most active. In all my years in the woods, I have only witnessed fourteen occasions of wild whitetail deer mating during daylight hours. However, I have observed hundreds of mating episodes of wild whitetail deer after darkness, during the nights of the full moon, over many years.

As I mentioned before, most deer usually travel to their daytime bedding areas within three hours or so after daylight, depending on weather conditions. During the rut, any sexually mature buck that did not pair up with a doe in estrous during the night usually beds down somewhere downwind of a master scrape, within an hour or so after daylight. There the buck waits until all the does of the herd, traveling on their own, separate trails toward their bedding sites in late morning, pass through the area of the herd's master scrape, and bed down for the day. Sometime after the does pass by the master scrape the mature buck usually leaves his bed and follows the does' trails to their various bedding sites, searching for any doe that may soon go into estrous. Then, if no does in heat are found in the bedding areas, the mature buck usually travels around on his scent trail, scent-checking the condition of his rubs and scrapes, to see if any doe in heat might have passed by one of his own scrapes. This is why you frequently see mature whitetail bucks traveling around in daylight conditions between the hours of ten a.m. and two p.m. during the rut. The unpaired, anxious, and frustrated bucks are traveling from bedding area to bedding area, from scrape to scrape, searching for does to mate. This is why you should not leave the woods at this time of day for your normal lunchtime meal if you're hunting for a trophy buck! In all my years of bowhunting and observing whitetail deer behavior, I have seen more trophy-class whitetail bucks traveling around between the hours of ten a.m. and two p.m., during the rut, than any other time frame.

After the mature buck finishes searching all of the herd's bedding areas for a doe in estrous, and scent-checking the condition of the rubs and scrapes on his territorial trail from his scent trail, he usually returns to his daytime bed somewhere downwind of the area of the herd's master scrape and waits for the does of the herd to leave their daytime bedding areas in the late afternoon or early evening. Then, once again, the mature buck follows the trails of the does after the does travel through and pass the area of the herd's master scrape toward their nighttime feeding areas. This cycle of behavior continues on for all sexually mature bucks of the herd throughout the primary rut and any re-

During the rut, bucks—even mature bucks—that are not paired up with a doe in heat travel around on their scent trails, scent-checking their rubs and scrapes.

curring estrous cycles of the does, until the buck is paired up with a doe in heat.

Master scrapes are more closely watched by the bucks of the herd during the hours of daylight, while the does are bedded down. When a big, mature herd buck's fresh, strong "musk scent" is in the area of the master scrape, the other bucks of the herd usually stay clear. They fear the herd buck, and his fresh scent there tells them that he is somewhere in the area. However, the other sexually mature, less dominant bucks of the herd will usually bed and travel somewhere downwind of a master scrape many times during the daylight hours to see if the big herd buck is still bedding in the area, and to scent-check the master scrape for any does in estrous that may have traveled past when the big buck was not in the area.

You should never hunt real close to a master scrape or your scent will be carried by the wind to the nose of any

The author with the largest-bodied buck ever taken in Maryland. Known as "big Moe," the buck was taken on his scent trail in late afternoon. Field-dressing 265 pounds, he carried an eight-point rack scoring 148 7/8 P&Y.

herd buck that travels downwind of the master scrape to scent-check it. Bucks typically lift their noses high up in the air to intensely scent-check any scrape, and if you were there, or your scent is on the ground nearby or anywhere around the scrape, the bucks will scent you downwind and spook. You should always hunt downwind of a master scrape, somewhere near and downwind of the mature buck's scent trail!

Sexually mature bucks make grunting noises whenever they approach a group of deer that has a doe in estrous with them or while they are following a doe's sex trail, and especially when they chase a doe around as part of the mating ritual. This grunting noise sounds very familiar to that of a grunting hog, at a slightly higher pitch in one to three second

Here's a whitetail buck that has just shed its antlers in early March. The pedicels or antler bases can be seen just forward of the ears.

intervals, and it serves to warn other less dominant bucks to stay clear. You can usually hear a buck making these grunting sounds from great distances away, as the buck approaches a doe in heat and runs her off away from other deer, or when a buck follows a doe's sex trail through the woods.

While you are hunting, if you happen to see a doe traveling through the woods followed in time by a grunting buck, immediately move yourself over, close to the area where the doe and buck have just passed. The doe is definitely in heat, and the grunting buck is following her sex trail. Any other bucks that travel anywhere near or through the same section of woods where the doe has previously traveled will scent her sex trail on the ground, and they will follow it wherever it leads. Sooner or later, any buck or bucks that are following that doe's sex trail will travel right through the same area where you saw the doe and buck earlier, and if you are there you will have a pretty good chance to take down a buck. You do not need a treestand. Just quickly move to a place downwind of where you saw the doe and buck traveling. Try to locate yourself behind some low brush, a tree stump, or anything else in the area that will partially conceal you from a buck's direct vision, and where your scent cannot be carried by the wind to the buck's nose before he reaches you. Most bucks that are following a doe's sex trail travel with their head and nose low to the ground, and they usually do not pay too much attention to anything else. So, unless you are moving around too much, or you smell too bad, or you are making too much noise, most bucks will not even notice you. I have seen as many as eight herd bucks following the same doe's sex trail through the woods within a two-hour period of time. Over the past years, I have killed many fine bucks by just quickly moving over to where I had seen a grunting buck following a doe's sex trail through the woods. It often takes about ten to fifteen minutes after the doe in heat until the first grunting buck passes by.

The number of does and breeding bucks within any deer herd determines how long the herd's primary breeding season or rut actually lasts. In most areas three weeks is generally considered to be the average duration. After all the does of a herd are bred, or they naturally stop experiencing their second heat cycle, the sexually mature bucks of the herd usually temporarily leave their herd's home range territory and their territorial breeding areas for days at a time, searching for any other does that may still be going into estrous in other deer herds. The high testosterone levels in their bodies still drive them to mate, and their nervous energy still compels them to travel around a lot.

When these lone, free-ranging mature bucks travel into other deer herds' home range territories they encounter and challenge the other herds' mature bucks for the breed-

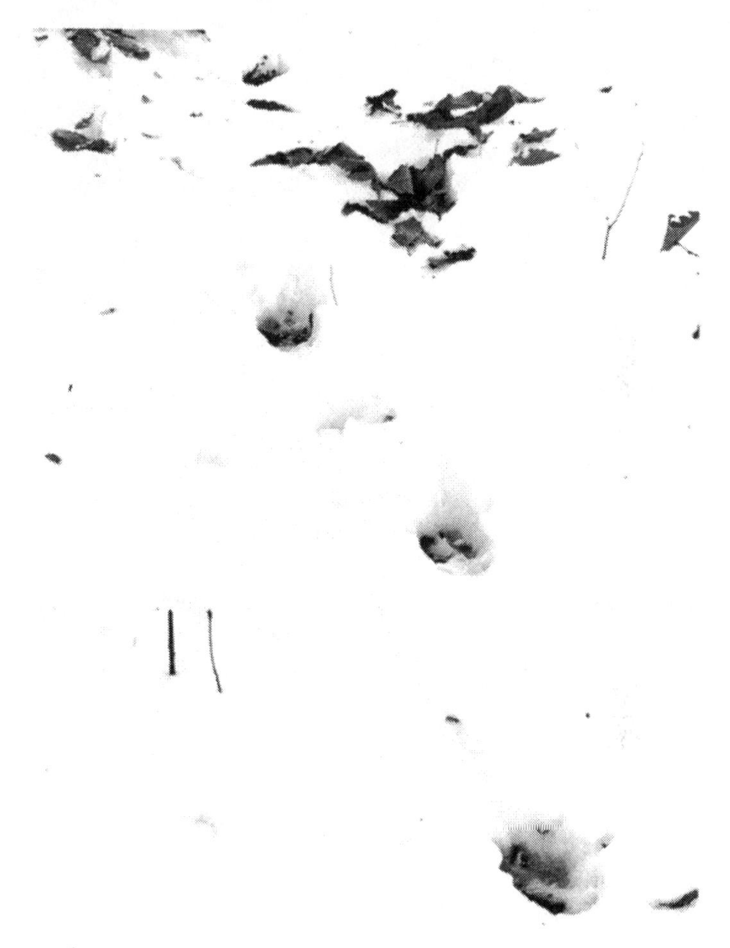

With practice the tracks of a mature whitetail buck can be easily recognized by the well-rounded front hooves and drag marks left in soft ground or snow.

ing rights of any does in their herd that are still in heat. These are usually the only times mature bucks actually fight each other in brutal combat. Most of the time, these roving, mature bucks try to establish their dominance over the other herd's mature bucks by a variety of different aggressive postures. Sometimes they just stare hard at each other, with their ears lowered down behind their heads, or they will raise their heads and antlers high in the air, each displaying the size of their antlers to intimidate the other buck. Other times, these rogue bucks may stand fully erect, broadside to one another, with the hair on their bodies raised up like angry dogs, to make them look bigger and more aggressive to the other buck. Mature bucks go through all types of aggressive behavior and postures before they ever actually engage in head-to-head combat. Most times, the smaller or the less aggressive buck of the two becomes submissive to the more aggressive buck, and the challenge ends quickly with the loser trotting away. However, mature bucks of different herds with the same physical size and stature occasionally battle it out head-to-head with each other. The winners of these physical, sometimes fatal contests win the breeding rights of any does in that herd that are still in estrous. If a free-ranging, mature buck is beaten and chased away from another herd's home range territory, the buck usually returns back to its own home range area and waits for the does of the herd to begin their third heat cycle. It occurs near the rising full moon in the early part of December, twenty-six to twenty-eight days after the doe's second estrous cycle ends. Once again, whitetail does living in the more southern latitudes experience their second estrous cycle and primary rut near the rising full moon in early to mid-December, and whitetail does living in the more northern latitudes experience their second estrous cycle and primary rut near the rising full moon in early to mid-October.

At just about the same time the does experience their second heat cycle the testosterone levels in a buck's body have risen to near peak conditions. Each time a buck mates with a doe and ejaculates he slightly lowers the testosterone levels in his body. The more a buck mates, the more testosterone is used. When testosterone levels fall to a certain critical low point, over a period of time, the buck's antlers weaken at the pedicel or base, and fall off. Since the big, mature bucks of the herd do most of the breeding, they usually shed their antlers weeks before the other bucks of the herd. The larger, breeding bucks usually shed their antlers in late December to mid-January if they did a lot of mating, while the smaller bucks normally shed their antlers in later February through the end of March. I have seen some young bucks still carrying their antlers during the first weeks of April. However, most whitetail deer have usually shed their antlers by late March.

Nature provides deer with great senses of hearing, smell, and vision, and the quickness and speed to elude most natural predators to survive. But deer have one flaw that nature overlooked. They leave droppings, tracks, and other signs of their existence wherever they live and travel, and that makes them very vulnerable to human hunters who can read their signs of life. And, that is the only reason why some deer can be successfully hunted!

The key to deer life is the lush, moist bottomlands that are surrounded by crop fields and forests, hills and mountains found within the deer herd's home range territory. Bottomland areas are the best places to begin looking for signs of deer life. Deer spend most of their nighttime lives traveling and feeding in and around these bottomland areas, and wherever the deer travel, they leave sign.

Deer walk and run on four very agile, muscular legs that are equipped with split hooves. This enables the deer to easily travel on or over all types of ground surfaces and terrain under most any weather condition, except ice. Deer are able to swim across large rivers, run up steep, rocky slopes of mountains, cross swampy marshlands, etc., on these very special, split hooves with little effort. However, the tracks left in soft ground areas can tell you much about the deer that made them.

The front hoof prints of a deer's tracks show you the sex and the size of the deer that made them. All deer begin life with small, pointed hooves, and as their bodies grow larger, their hooves naturally grow larger. But, as bucks and does grow older, their hooves wear differently, and their tracks will show you the difference. Does are usually smaller than bucks of the same age, and they are generally much smaller than mature bucks. Does have much smaller neck and shoulder areas than bucks, which transfer less mass weight down their front legs to their hooves. Does are very feminine and dainty and when they walk they lift each front foot completely off the ground. This causes their front hooves to wear very little, so their hooves usually remain very pointed. Bucks are much heavier in the neck and shoulder areas, which transfers more mass weight down their front legs to their hooves. Especially a heavily muscled, swollen necked mature buck carrying a large set of heavy antlers during the rut. This causes the bucks to slightly drag their front hooves when they walk. Over a period of time, as their bodies grow larger and heavier, the bucks wear down the pointed tips of their hooves into blunt, rounded shapes. You can easily see the difference and the drag marks made by a large buck's front hooves in soft, moist ground or snow. The larger and heavier a buck grows, the more rounded his front hooves become.

The length and width of an average buck's front hoof is also usually slightly larger than an average doe's, but the rear hooves of full grown, mature deer are generally about the same size, unless they belong to an exceptionally large deer of either sex. And, all deer have "dew claws" on their

The author with a very large doe whose tracks fooled him—she had big hooves on all four feet and she dressed out at 172 pounds, a Maryland record.

feet. I once killed a very large doe that dressed out at 172 pounds. She had very large, pointed front hooves and very large rear hooves. I was slightly confused by the size and shape of this particular deer's tracks. I first found them while I was still-hunting during the rut that year. While tracking this deer two days later, I stalked to within shooting distance. I killed this large deer while it was feeding in a honeysuckle thicket so thick that I could not see its head while it was down feeding. By the size of the deer's large body that I *could* see, and the large tracks that I had followed, I naturally assumed that this deer was a large buck. When I walked up to the deer lying dead on the ground, I was shocked to see that it was a very large doe instead of a buck. I learned that day to judge all deer by the shape and size of their front hooves, and not their rear hooves!

Deer droppings or pellets also show you where deer live, and where they traveled. The size of the pellets will show you the size of the deer that dropped them. The larger the

All large whitetail deer have big rear hooves. These tracks in a dry streambed were made by a buck weighing between 250 and 280 pounds, live weight. The binoculars measure five by seven inches.

pellets, the larger the deer. Large does and large bucks both have large vents, or anal openings, and they both drop large pellets. However, bucks usually drop larger pellets because they are normally bigger animals.

When you find fresh deer droppings, break them open, smell them, and look to see what the deer have been feeding on. Their odor, color, and texture will show you what the deer have been eating. If you can determine what the deer are eating, you can narrow down the types of areas where those foods are found, and better locate the trails leading to those feeding areas. If you see a lot of green color inside their pellets, the deer are probably still grazing on grasses, etc., and if they are more brownish, the deer are browsing. If the pellets are dark brown and they have a strong, bark odor to them, the deer are probably feeding on acorns. The more often you break open deer pellets to see and smell what they are eating, the better you will be at determining what they ate. It comes from experience!

Deer pellets are moist and soft, and glisten when they are real fresh. Within twenty-four hours the outer covering of the pellets usually becomes dull in appearance and somewhat firm to the touch, and over a longer period of time they slowly decay away.

Sometimes you can tell which way a deer was traveling and what the wind direction was when the deer defecated, by the way the pellets lie on the ground. When a deer defecates while it is walking, more pellets fall in the beginning of the bowel movement than at the end. The area of droppings that contains the least amount of pellets usually points the direction the deer was walking, and the general direction of the wind when that deer was there. Many times deer drop their pellets while they are standing still, feeding, etc., and it is hard to figure out which direction the deer were traveling. But if the pellets are fresh and glistening, you can always check a local newspaper's forecast to see what the wind conditions were for the past couple of days. From that information, you can determine what the wind direction was, and the direction the deer was traveling when it dropped the pellets.

CHAPTER SEVEN

SCENT CONTROL AND CAMOUFLAGE

Humans rarely use their sense of smell or olfactory system except for occasionally sniffing at some of their favorite foods cooking in the kitchen, or other strong, nasty odors floating by in the air around them. Most humans are usually totally unaware of all the subtle scents found in and on the things they handle and use every day in their lives because they just do not take the time to sniff them. The use of all the personal cleaning items, gasolines, household chemicals, etc., used regularly in our daily lives tends to dull or overpower our sense of smell to a level that makes most subtle odors undetectable. And, anything that humans cannot easily smell is generally considered by humans to be odorless, and naturally overlooked.

In this next section of the book I want to explain to you how humans overlook the deer's great sense of smell, and show you how to change some of your bad hunting habits. If you want to get close to deer, you have to beat their nose. The way you beat their nose is to eliminate all possible odors from your clothing, your boots, your equipment, and your body.

Preferably you should have at least two complete sets of hunting clothing, including all your underwear, socks, T-shirts, or whatever else you normally wear when you hunt. You should wear some type of camouflage clothing or some other dark, dull colored clothing that has definite lines or patterns to help break up the shape and outline of your body. The darker shades of camouflage clothing work the best. The lighter shades of camouflage clothing are just too bright in the woods after the leaves fall, and they are much too obvious to the deer and other animals of the woods.

Wash all your hunting clothes in just plain, cold water and hang them out in trees and bushes or in the woods for a few days or so to dry and air out. Rub some dry leaves and twigs found on the ground in the woods all over your hunting clothes. Put some of these leaves and twigs in all the pockets and hats, etc., to add some real "woods" smell to them. The smell of the "woods" in and on your hunting clothing helps to mask the natural odor of your body when you hunt.

The reason you should have two complete sets of hunting clothing is that while you are wearing one set to hunt in, the other set, already aired out, is ready for the next day's hunt. You should rotate your hunting clothes each time you hunt, so that you always have fresh, "woods scented" clothing on when you hunt. While you are wearing one set, the other set should be out hanging in the woods, airing out, to remove any odors they picked up and absorbed when you last hunted. Stinky, smelly clothes spook deer.

Also, wash and air out two pairs of mosquito net camouflage gloves, and two mosquito net camouflaged headnets. Once again, rub leaves, etc., on these items to help add a "woodsy" smell to them.

You must wear some type of camouflage on your face and hands. The light to dark skin colors of a human's face and hands tend to brightly shine out in the woods during dark and daylight conditions, especially those of the Caucasian race. If you have never seen a human in the woods without camouflage on their face and hands, take my word on it, they stand out like glowing objects, and deer can definitely see them.

Many of today's hunters use camouflage creams on their face and hands, and they do an excellent job of camouflaging. However, many of these products will leave chemical odors on your skin and on any clothing they touch. If you, I, or your dog or cat can smell them, the deer can smell them. Some day, sooner or later, they will cost you a nice buck, because he smelled them. Try washed out, camouflaged, mosquito netting. It works!

I have heard some hunters complain about wearing the mosquito net material headnets and gloves. They say "that the mosquito net material is just too scratchy or rough on their skin," or that "they cannot see too clearly through the mosquito net material." Those minor problems are easily solved. When you first wash out the "new" smell of your headnet and gloves with just plain, cold water, the mosquito net material becomes soft and subtle. And after they air out and dry, if you just roll the headnet and gloves back and forth between your hands a few times, they become as soft as smooth toilet paper. For better vision, just cut out enough of the netting material around the area of the eyes so that you can see clearly, or buy the headnets that are manufactured with eye holes already cut in them. Then cut out the strip of material that separates the eye holes from each other and you will have clean, unobstructed vision.

Once your deer hunting clothes have been aired out in the woods, do not wear any of these clothes for anything other than hunting. During the hunting season, when you are not out hunting leave these clothes hanging out in the woods, airing out, or store each complete set separately in large plastic trash bags. Be sure to wash out the plastic trash bags with plain, cold water and air them out, to get the industrial smell out of them before you put your fresh, aired out hunting clothes in them. Otherwise, your hunting clothes will smell like plastic trash bags. You are trying to remove odors, not put them in!

Buy yourself a new pair of cool-weather hunting boots—any brand that has the leather uppers and rubber bottoms. The ones with the removable wool liners are the best. If you have to hunt in the mid-to-warm weather occasionally, a second pair of the lightweight style of these boots would be a good investment. Also, buy yourself a pair of replacement boot liners for your new boots; you will use them as spares. The extra boot liners are used just like the second set of hunting clothes. While you are wearing one pair, the other pair should be airing out for the next day's hunt. Deer can smell stinky boot liners, too!

Rubber bottom boots will keep your feet warm and dry, and they are the only type of footwear I know of that leaves no scent on the ground when they are clean. Leather hunting boots, or work boots, absorb and hold foot odors and perspiration. Each time you wear them they accumulate more sweat and foot odor, and you can never remove it. Tennis shoes or sneakers are even worse. If you and I can smell them, the deer can smell them. Deer can pick up the scented trail of a human who is wearing leather boots or tennis shoes on dry ground sixty to ninty minutes, or longer, after the trail was left. Believe it! I personally like the "Sorel" boots made by Kaufman. I have tried all other types of boots over the past years, and the Sorel's are the only boots that have ever kept my feet warm, dry, and comfortable, in all types of weather.

Wash your boots and all the liners in plain, cold water and set them out in the woods to dry and air out. It is also a good idea to break in your new boots by walking in them

Of all the senses of the whitetail, his nose is the most difficult to defeat.

in the woods. While you are walking through the woods, step into all the creeks and streams you can find, and walk along their muddy banks. This all helps to remove the odors of the new leather and rubber from the boots, and replaces it with the scent of the woods.

You should never wear your deer hunting boots for anything other than hunting deer. Never! If it is at all possible, never put your hunting boots on until you arrive at the woods where you are going to hunt. Many hunters stop to pick up snacks or other goodies to carry with them while they hunt, or they stop to put gas in their car or truck on the way to their hunting areas. If they happen to step on any motor oil, antifreeze, bubble gum, spilled soda, coffee, or anything else that lies all over the ground in these types of areas, they will contaminate the soles of their boots with strong, everlasting odors. Needless to say, deer do not use any of these items in their daily life and they will scent them anywhere you walk or stand in the woods. So, think twice before you put your feet, and your boots, down on the ground anywhere. You may spoil a good day's hunt, and you could ruin a good pair of hunting boots forever!

If you use portable treestands, make sure you wash them off with plain, cold water, and set them up in the woods to dry and air out. If they have been recently painted or camouflaged, leave them out in the woods for two to three weeks before you ever use them. Throw leaves and twigs all over them, and if possible, let the rain shower them a couple of times. It all helps to get rid of the paint and metal smell.

Do not carry anything into the woods with you that you do not absolutely need. Anything you carry will have a certain amount of scent to it, and the deer could smell it. Anything that you wear, use, or carry with you needs to be washed clean of odors and aired out before you take it to the woods. Especially items such as new leather knife sheaths, cargo belts, plastic canteens, etc. Anything that you carry in your hip pouch or fanny pack, such as first aid items, compass, survival gear, etc., should be put into plastic, resealable bags to prevent the deer from scenting them, or they will. These plastic bags also need to be washed and aired out.

If you smoke cigarettes in your car or truck on the way to your hunting area, do not wear your hunting clothing in the vehicle, even if you keep your windows open while you are driving. Your clothing will absorb the smoke odors, and deer will smell them. You should leave your hunting clothes in the plastic trash bags until after you arrive where you are going to hunt, then put them on.

I do not recommend that anyone smoke while they are hunting deer. But, if you must, carry a small, plastic, watertight container that is filled just about half full of water. Put all your ashes and your cigarette butts in this container, and lock in their nasty odors with the waterproof cap. Nothing stinks worse than a cigarette butt that has been snuffed out on the bark of a tree and left there. Deer will smell it and you at the same time. If you leave it there, after you leave the woods the deer will smell it, they will remember where it was, and they will scent-check that area whenever they pass through.

Should you ever smoke a cigarette while you are hunting, let the wind carry the smoke up away from you, so that it does not settle on you or your clothing and taint them. Smoke only at times when the wind or the thermals will carry the smoke upwards, away from the low, ground areas and the deer's nose. Keep your hand and head movements to a minimum, your eyes and ears open, and always be ready to douse your cigarette in your watertight container.

I don't personally believe in using man-made or collected cover scents such as "fox urine," "skunk," "acorn," "apple blossom," etc. Deer are not particularly fond of foxes or skunks. I do not know of anything in the woods that likes the smell of skunk, except maybe another skunk. And, I have seen enough foxes chase, kill, and eat fawns to convince me that deer are not really fond of "fox scent." I believe that the use of these products releases strange odors into the air, broadcasting to the deer exactly where you are located. A deer that scents them knows that something is wrong. Deer are instantly alerted to anything that is out of place. The whole idea of a perfect ambush, and the purpose of hunting clean, is to try to prevent the deer from even knowing that anything is in the area!

Your body is the source of the most offending odors to deer. You are what you eat and drink—and you smell like what you eat and drink. To slip the deer's nose, you are going to have to change your eating habits and change your bathing methods before you hunt, and while you are hunting.

At least two days before you go hunting, do not use any soaps, shampoos, underarm deodorants, toothpaste, after-shaves, or any other cosmetic items on your body. They all leave chemical residues and odors on your body, and nothing in the woods smells like them. Deer do not use them, and neither should you. You can wash and clean your body, teeth, and hair, with just plain water. A daily shower with just plain, clean water will generally remove any dirt and odor from your external body, and leave it smelling clean and natural.

Do not take baths, no matter how clean the tub is. There is always chemical residue left on the surfaces of a bathtub from the soaps, shampoos, etc., that were used previously, and they will just be transferred onto your body while you soak in the water. You may not be able to smell them because your nose is accustomed to these scents, a deer's nose is not. A soapless bath in a clear, running creek or stream is always refreshing, and naturally cleansing!

What you eat and drink two days before you hunt affects how your body smells while you hunt. Do not eat Chinese, Italian, Mexican, or any other foods that use spices like garlic, oregano, onion, etc. These spices, and their odors, stay in your body for a couple of days and when you breathe or perspire, their pungent odors are passed out through your skin, onto your clothing, and into the air around you wherever you go. Deer do not eat them, and they are not used to the smell of them. So you should not eat them before you go hunting deer or their odors will spook the deer.

No matter what efforts you go through to try to keep your body clean and odor free, inside and out, there is always going to be some human body odor present. But, that can be easily covered. While I don't personally use com-

The author believes the best cover scents are natural food sources found in your hunting area; if you're hunting near an apple orchard, use only the apples that grow there.

mercial cover scents, I certainly believe in cover scents! There are many, many wild plants and trees that grow in the woods and fields where you hunt with natural odors that are strong enough to mask your natural body scent when it is clean. These cover scents will not spook the deer if used properly and they cost absolutely nothing. I use them when I bowhunt, and I have killed many big, 200-pound-class whitetail bucks using them while still-hunting and stalking. Nature offers them to you and they work!

To me, the best types of cover scents are the leaves and fruit products of the plants and trees that deer feed on. The fruit products are the berries, nuts, acorns, etc. They all have a distinct scent to them. They will mask your natural body odor while you hunt, and they will not spook the deer. Deer find their food with their noses, not their eyes. If you smell like the food that the deer are eating, they are not going to scent you and the deer are not going to expect any danger while they are eating.

It is very important that you use the proper food cover scent for the area that you are hunting. You have to use a little common sense! If you are hunting in an area where the deer are currently feeding on polk berries, do not use the scent of white oak acorns as your cover scent or the deer are going to know that something is wrong. The white oak acorn scent will be out of place, and the deer will know it.

When you use the deer's natural food for your cover scent, you need to put it on your clothes, on your body, and all over the ground, all around the immediate area where you are hunting. You want to smell like the deer's food, but you do not want to be the only source of the fresh, food scent in that area. Otherwise, you will draw all the attention of the deer's nose to the fresh food scent on you.

If you plan to use acorns to mask your scent, pick up a handful or so off the ground from the area where you are going to hunt. Cut a few of them in half and rub the meat from these acorns on your face, hands, and clothing. Then cut the rest of them up into small pieces, and throw them out away from you, as far as you can, scattering them out all over the ground in all directions around you. This spreads the fresh scent of acorns over a much larger area and directly away from you. Any deer that come into this area to feed smell the acorns that are scattered out all over the ground, and not just the ones rubbed on you.

White oak acorns are much sweeter to the taste than other species of acorns, and they are the preferred, first choice for food for deer in the woods during early fall. Deer always seek out and feed in the areas of the woods that contain white oak trees, and the scent of the white oak acorns is an excellent cover scent.

Any time you use acorns, beechnuts, hickory nuts, etc., as your cover scent, use them in the same manner that I have just described to you. You do not really need to use a lot of food scent to mask your body and hunting clothes. Their natural odors are usually strong enough to cover your clean, natural body scent, and using a lot of food scent does not really make the cover scent any stronger. It only concentrates most of the food scent odor on you rather than the area that you're hunting.

CHAPTER EIGHT

USING COVER SCENTS; BOWHUNTING PRINCIPLES

If you plan to hunt near the edge or in the middle of dense honeysuckle or greenbriar thickets, walk a twenty to twenty-five yard radius circle around the spot you plan to hunt. As you slowly walk around the circle, stop here and there and break off some leaves and pieces of the vines and rub them all over your face, hands, and clothing. Put the remains of these crushed leaves and pieces of vines in your pockets, on your hat, in your boot laces, etc., to mask your body scent. The purpose of walking the circle out around the spot you plan to hunt and breaking off pieces of leaves and vines here and there is to release fresh natural food scent into the air all around the area you are hunting. This will not usually spook the deer if your feet are clean, because when deer walk around and feed in these types of areas, they release fresh, natural, food scent into the air all around them as they nibble off parts of these plants. The deer are used to the fresh, food scent in the air all around them in these types of areas and it helps you prevent the deer's nose from homing in on the fresh, natural food scent that is rubbed on you.

If you plan to hunt in or near the edge of an apple orchard, use the apples from the trees where you are hunting as your cover scent. Not all apples have the same scent. If you buy red delicious apples from the store and try to use them to cover your scent in an orchard of winesap or crab apple trees, the deer will know something is wrong. They will smell the difference and spook. Use only what grows in the area where you hunt to cover your scent!

I rub the leaves and branches of spicebush on me and my clothing whenever I hunt in the low, bottomland areas. It naturally grows in these types of areas. It has a sweet, strong, spice odor and deer like to eat it occasionally and they have never scented me when I have used it. I have stalked up to and killed many whitetail bucks while they were sleeping in their beds using spicebush as my cover scent. It is one of the best cover scents to use, and one of my favorites!

If you hunt in the woods in or around the salt marsh swamps of the eastern United States, use the leaves and twigs of bay leaf bushes that naturally grow in these areas as your cover scent. They have a very strong odor that will easily cover your scent, especially if you crumble up the leaves. Any deer that live in these areas are used to its ever-present smell, and it will not spook them. I killed one of my largest whitetail bucks using bay leaves as my cover scent, while bow hunting in a salt marsh area along the Chesapeake Bay. I shot him at a distance of less than eight feet while I was standing behind a small group of bay leaf bushes. He passed by me with the wind to his back, and was unable to scent me *downwind*, at this close distance. Now this very large, ten-point buck, dressing out at 221 pounds, adorns my wall thanks to the natural odor of bay leaves. It does the trick!

Pine, spruce, cedar, mountain laurel, sassafras, etc., are all good, strong cover scents that will not spook the deer if used properly. No matter where you hunt there is always something available that naturally grows in the areas that will cover your clean body scent. All you have to do is use them!

You need to use a little thought and common sense when it comes to which cover scent you use when you hunt for deer in one area in the morning and you hunt for deer in a different area in the evening during the same day. If you used honeysuckle to mask your body scent in the morning and then you decide to hunt in the oaks in the evening, you are going to have to change your clothes and wash your face and hands to remove your morning cover scent or you will spook the deer that come to feed in the oaks.

If you plan to hunt in vastly different feeding places during the same day, do not rub the food cover scent directly on your clothing and body. Instead, just hang or lay a few pieces of whatever you use to mask your body scent close by and out around you on small tree branches or anything else that will hold the scent pieces, so that their fresh scent goes into the air all around you. This is not the best way to use cover scents, but it saves you having to change your clothes twice a day.

As I mentioned before, many hunters stop and pick up snacks to carry with them while they hunt; or, they stop to have breakfast or coffee before they go hunting. This is one bad habit you should stop when you go hunting. When you go into these stores, restaurants, or breakfast bars, you are going to pick up and absorb very strong, greasy bacon and egg–type odors that cling to your body, your hair, and your clothing. Even if you put your hunting clothes on after you eat breakfast, you are still going to smell like breakfast foods. The odors are already on your skin and in your hair. Coffee and breakfast foods also put odors in your stomach and throat and when you breathe, these strong odors flow out of your mouth and nose like a cook's chimney. With these greasy odors and all the cigarette smoke that lingers in these areas on you, you are going to smell like one stinking critter to the deer. It makes no sense to clean your body, air out your clothing, drive two to three hours to hunt, and go into the woods smelling like eggs and bacon or coffee. You are just wasting your time. Deer are going to smell you!

The odor from breakfast foods is not the only problem you have when you eat before you hunt. Two to three hours or less after you eat these greasy foods and drink coffee you are going to have to urinate and defecate. More than likely you will probably have to relieve yourself after only being in the woods for an hour or so during prime hunting time. When you do finally relieve yourself you are going to leave a powerful scent on the ground and in the air and the deer are going to smell it for days. Even if you relieve yourself in a plastic bag and carry it out of the woods with you, you still have to go through all the motions of hanging your equipment up somewhere, dropping your pants, squatting, etc., and all the movements of redressing, etc. During this time while you are moving and scenting the woods, deer could see you moving or scent you downwind and your morning hunt would be over. It seems to me that it would be much easier and more practical to not eat or drink anything before you hunt. I really do not believe that anyone would ever die of starvation by missing breakfast before they hunt. For those of you that insist on carrying snacks and candy bars while you hunt, put them in washed out, resealable, plastic sandwich bags so the deer cannot smell them or they will.

You must understand that deer have learned to associate these particular odors and sounds with that of danger. Whitetail deer have been taught these scents of danger by thousands of previous hunters over the past years. Many hunters in the past, and many still today, traditionally have camped near or on their hunting lands a day or two before the hunting season opened. They cooked their meals and

This mature whitetail—188 pounds dressed weight—was taken while using pungent spicebush as the cover scent. If spicebush grows where you're hunting it's a good choice for cover scent.

coffee and put all the scent of these foods, including all the vehicle noise and odors, directly in the fields and woods around where they were going to hunt. Many of the deer learned to associate these particular scents and sounds with danger; they have been hunted or pressured to move by man soon after these odors and sounds appeared. The deer that survived these types of hunting situations passed their learned, life experiences on to other generations of deer by immediately spooking and running away in panic whenever these offending odors or sounds appeared in the air again. Any other deer of the herd that sees an older, wiser deer run away when these strange odors appear instinctively learns to do the same. This is one of the main reasons why most deer taken by hunters are less than one and a half years of age. The young deer have not yet learned that these odors and sounds are the signs of man and danger. The older deer have, and they run far from the area to survive.

Everything that I have explained to you so far is basically what I believe you really need to know about deer to hunt them. If you understand what I have been saying, you should realize by now that deer movement is very predictable, and that it is all controlled by the direction of the wind, the weather, and daylight conditions. You should understand, and know why, and where, deer generally like to bed under all types of conditions. You should know enough about natural deer behavior to understand why, and how, they react to various situations that affect their lives and survival. And, you should be ready to understand how to hunt them.

When you step into the woods to hunt you enter the deer's world, a world that very few humans could survive in twenty-four hours a day, 365 days a year. This is a world that most humans do not know anything about, except what they read in magazines. You come to hunt the deer in their world in the morning and you leave the woods at dark, when deer are the most active. You are limited to the amount of time you can actually hunt because of your work and family commitments. You can probably only hunt on Saturdays and the holidays if you are lucky. If you are really one of the lucky ones, you can probably take a week, or two weeks, off from your job to go hunting—if you did not use all of your vacation time to go fishing, or take your family to Disney World, etc.

If you hunt every weekend, you can probably make it to the woods to hunt deer only about fifteen to twenty days a year. And that is only possible if the bowhunting season in your state runs from the beginning of September to the end of January. Even then that is only possible if you do not have to use any of your weekends to attend any weddings or family gatherings or take the kids somewhere for their weekend activities. If you were able to hunt every weekend during the season for the past ten years, you would still have less time in the woods than a yearling deer, including all your scouting time. And, for those reasons alone, you are going to need all the "right" information and all the bowhunting tricks you can get your hands on just to kill a deer, much less a P&Y trophy buck. Otherwise, you are just spending time in the woods, hoping to get lucky. Luck is for rabbits!

I have often heard friends of mine and many other hunters, say "Well, I did not see any deer, but I did see a couple of squirrels and I felt good getting out in the woods for a day." To me, this is just an excuse and a human's way of gracefully saying, "I failed." If they were really out hunting for food to survive, they would probably starve to death. They have the wrong attitude for hunting because they really do not know what they are doing, and they are just playing a game. They do not have their minds "right" for hunting. They go to the woods with "kill" on their mind, and they come home with fresh air in their lungs, and pacify themselves with stories of seeing squirrels. If they applied this same attitude and outlook to their jobs and work, they would probably be fired! When you put razor sharp broadheads on the end of your arrows and you enter the woods to hunt, your only purpose is to kill. If all you want to do is smell the fresh air, experience the woods, and see wildlife, then leave your bow at home and carry a camera with you. You will accomplish the same thing. You will have all the same great feelings without the "guilt of failure" hanging over your head to explain to your wife and friends. You have got to get your mind "right" for hunting.

I have heard many people refer to bowhunting as a sport. Well, it is not! It is a method of hunting and killing an animal. Archery is the sport! Many of the people who try hunting for deer and other big game animals with the bow and arrow nowadays are in it for the wrong reasons. Some try bowhunting mainly because their friends are trying it. And, there are always the few that say they bowhunt because, "they like the challenge of the 'one-on-one' type of hunting because it gives the deer a better chance." These people are usually the ones who hunt from treestands all the time and they could just as easily hunt a deer from their treestands "one-on-one" with a rifle. They do not really need to carry a bow in their hands to accomplish that feat. I have never heard any of these same people say that while they were out still-hunting through the woods, they stalked in close and killed a deer while it was sleeping in its bed!

The real reason that most people try bowhunting for deer simply is that they do not get their deer during the firearms season and, most of these people believe that if they hunt the longer bowhunting season, they will have much more time to hunt and get their deer. Well, they do have a much longer hunting season, but hunting deer with the bow and arrow is a "brand-new world," and most of them are still using "yesterday's maps." Most of them still do not get their deer with a bow and they are wondering why!

There are good days to hunt for deer and there are bad days to hunt for deer. There are good days to hunt from treestands and there are better days to still-hunt. Since most hunters are limited to hunting only on the weekends during the bow season, you need to know when the best times are for hunting, and for treestands, and understand why. Otherwise, you could be just wasting your very limited hunting time and effort, for years.

Ever since the early seventies treestand hunting has become deer hunting for most people, mainly because it is the easiest way for humans to hunt. It requires less physical energy and time to hunt from treestands and since most

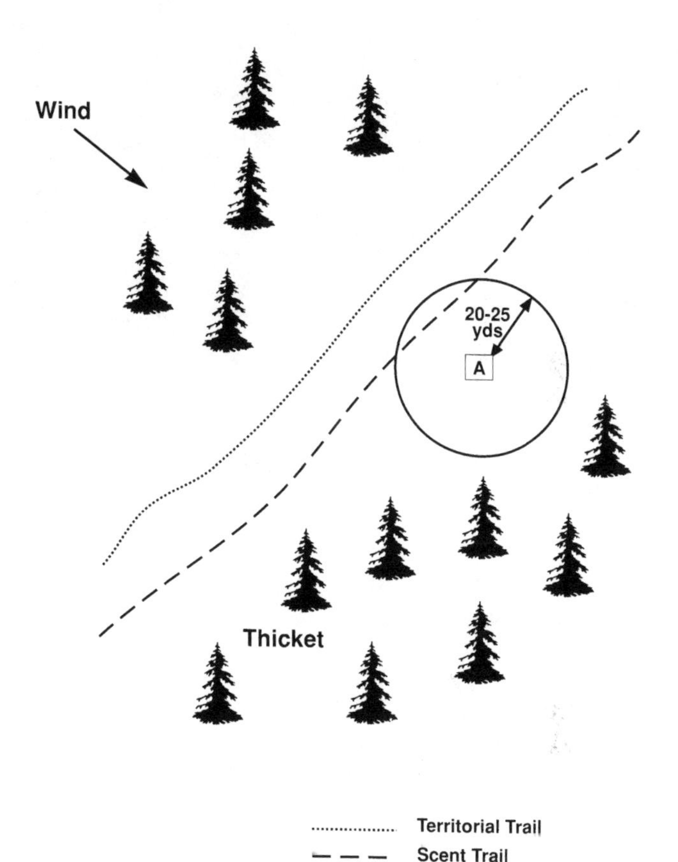

To use natural cover scent, walk a circle twenty to twenty-five yards radius from your treestand or ambush site A and break off and crush leaves and cones.

humans are basically lazy, they always seek out the easiest ways to do anything, including hunt deer. But you should understand that there are advantages to using treestands and there are many disadvantages.

Treestands will enable you to get above the low ground vegetation, which will allow you to have better visibility over a certain area. Treestands will also help you keep your

Bay leaf, another favorite of the author where it occurs, was the cover scent that helped fool this 221-pound ten-point in a tidal marshland area.

scent off the ground directly above where you are hunting. But treestands will limit the area you can actually hunt with your bow. For most people, it is only about a twenty-yard radius around the tree their stand is fastened to, if they are in an open area of woods.

If you still-hunt the woods and scout for fresh deer sign all day, you will cover a much larger section of woods and you will be able to discover where the deer are bedding, feeding, and traveling under various climatic and wind conditions. And, you will probably see a lot more game while you are out walking around hunting a large section of woods than you will generally see hunting over one spot from a treestand all day. Treestands will get your body scent up off the ground, but if you smell like a pile of dirty clothes, your being 10 or 30 feet off the ground is not really going to stop the deer from scenting you downwind. And your climbing up a tree is not going to remove your scent from the ground where you walked to the tree, especially if you wore a pair of dirty, stinky boots.

Many people build treestands in the woods and they habitually go to them to hunt just because they are there, or because their uncle shot a buck out of that particular stand last year. Regardless of the wind direction or other climatic conditions, they will hunt from these treestands day after day, weekend after weekend, while they are missing out on what is happening in other areas of the woods. There is a time and place to use treestands and that comes when you have located the exact place where you want to ambush your deer. You should set up your portable treestand the morning you hunt and take it out of the woods that night when you leave. Do not build a permanent treestand there or leave your portable there too long. If you do, sooner or later the deer will find your stand, your scent, or your tracks, and they will look for you each time they come through that area.

If a deer sees you up in a treestand and it does not spook and run away immediately, you have two options to consider before that deer circles you downwind and learns your scent. You must either kill the deer, even if it is a small doe, or never hunt in that same area again as long as that same deer is alive. If you do not kill that deer, it will become increasingly more curious and nervous about you. Eventually it will circle downwind of you and find your scent path, and it will learn, and know forever, the scent of you and know whenever you are in the woods again. If you do not kill that deer, its second sense will be triggered when it crosses your scent path downwind. It will spook and scent the area with its metatarsal glands, and your hunting in that area of the woods will be over for the day. Any other deer that comes near that "scented area" later on will know that something is wrong there and they also will avoid that area.

CHAPTER NINE

TREESTAND HUNTING; SEX LURES

If you do not kill that deer, it will look for you every time it comes through that area of the woods and if you are there it will more than likely ruin another day's hunt for you—especially if it crosses your scent path downwind. Deer remember where they saw a human in a tree, and they will always check out those areas before they will ever cross through them again. Many times after a deer sees a hunter in a tree the deer will shift its trail or shift its travel over to another herd trail that is located extremely far downwind, to better scent-check the area. Any other deer that follow that deer through that area in the future will know that something is wrong by that deer's alert behavior. Its constant nosing of the air and nervous body movements alert any other deer that are traveling near it, or with it, that something may be wrong or that something bad happened there before. Especially if you shot at the deer and missed it or wounded it. By seeing the alert deer's reactions in this particular area, the other deer instinctively learn to be cautious whenever they travel through this area. And now, every time these other deer come through this same area, they will check it out for themselves. If you ever hunt in that area again and any of these deer come through that area, they will look for you and they will find you every time.

You will make a big mistake if you do not kill a deer when it sees you in a treestand. You taught it where you hunt and how you hunt. By allowing that deer to live, it will, in time, teach other deer to look for you in that area. The choice is yours. Either kill the deer that saw you in your treestand and stop the other deer of the herd from learning your scent and where you hunt, or do not hunt that area again. You cannot have it both ways!

When you do use a treestand while you are hunting, do not sit down or hang your bow up while you wait for the deer to come. Sooner or later you are going to be caught sitting down and it may cost you a shot at a fine buck. One day a deer will seemingly appear out of nowhere, real close to you. While you are struggling to slowly and quietly stand up, reaching for your bow at the same time, the deer will pass by you or see you and spook. All you will be able to do is watch it go by, because you got caught sitting on your butt. You will remember that situation the rest of your hunting life. Most bow hunters need to experience this situation one time to really learn this lesson!

You cannot control what happens in the woods, or when. All you can do is wait, watch, and stay ready to shoot an arrow at the first opportune moment. You are only going to be there for a few hours at a time, and you want to be ready. You have gone through a lot of time and effort preparing yourself to hunt, and you have probably driven a couple of hours to get to the woods to hunt, so don't waste your time sitting on your tail. All the motions you go through to stand up or to reach for your bow when you need it—plus the time it takes to do all of this—will either prevent you from getting an arrow off at the deer or will spook the deer and possibly ruin your day's hunt.

When you do use portable treestands you don't really need to get any higher off the ground than about eight to ten feet. A deer's normal straight-line vision is only two to three feet above the ground. And, unless you are moving around too much or you stink too bad, the deer will usually never notice you or look for you up in a tree. Many times I use a non-climbing, portable treestand when I hunt, and I install it on a tree as high as I can reach and pull myself up on it. I have killed—and let more deer pass by me and under me—than most deer hunters ever see in their lifetime. You do not need to climb twenty feet in the air to kill deer. All you are doing by climbing that high up a tree is making a lot of excess, out-of-place noise in the woods and increasing the distance you may fall to the ground. Not to mention the fact that you are creating more difficult bow shots for yourself by shooting down at the deer at sharper angles, which makes deer much smaller targets to hit.

The normal width of a deer's back and rib cage is only about twelve to fourteen inches wide and the chest is only about sixteen to eighteen inches high. When you are at a distance of twenty feet above the ground and the deer is fifteen to twenty-five yards away from you, the deer's back will appear to be only about four to six inches wide, and the chest area will appear to be only about ten to twelve inches high. If the deer is moving out away from you the back and chest areas are going to appear even smaller. These conditions create a much smaller target area for you to hit with an arrow, and that is one of the reasons why many bow hunters miss or wound the deer they shoot at.

When you set up your portable treestand you should always try to select a tree that has a few branches on it, or pick out a tree that is large enough in diameter to hide your body's silhouette from the deer's vision when you stand up against it. The leaves and branches on the tree, near and around you help you blend into the shape of the tree. And, if you crumble up some of the leaves or break open a couple of small branches, they will help to mask your body scent with that of the tree.

If you set your stand up in the open woods on a bare tree you are going to stand out like a telephone repairman perched on a telephone pole on the side of a road. You will be much too visible and any deer that gets close to you will probably see you whenever you do move. Under certain conditions you can set your stand on a bare, limbless tree, but that should be only when you have a lot of other trees with leaves or some other type of foliage directly in your background or around you and when you are not profiled against the skyline. However, you should be totally covered with camouflage material, especially your face and hands, and you must be very still and very slow in your movements for this setup to be effective. Otherwise, you will stand out like a duck flapping its wings if you just reach up to scratch your head.

When you do set up your treestand to hunt, try to walk a straight-line path directly to the tree you plan to use. By doing this you disturb much less ground area as you walk. This leaves much less fresh, disturbed ground scent in the air and on the ground near the area where deer could possibly walk before they reach the area where your treestand is located. When you put your treestand up, try to locate your stand in the most downwind location of the area you plan to hunt. If possible, try to set your stand at least fifteen to twenty yards downwind of the trail or the area where you expect the deer to be traveling through—especially along the edge of rivers, woods, or marshlands that connect large areas. This is where deer like to travel; it's their safest route.

Whenever possible always try to situate your stand on

A deer's normal straight-line vision is only two to three feet above the ground. Depending on the terrain, the author believes you don't need to put your treestand higher than eight to ten feet off the ground.

the tree with the sun to your back. That way, if a deer should ever look up toward you it will be looking into the sun, and the deer will not be able to see you as clearly as normal. You need to use a little common sense and take advantage of any situation you can when you are hunting from a treestand. You have to because once you are set up to hunt, you cannot easily move to another tree without the possibility of ruining your morning or evening hunt.

Most of the time treestand hunters are strictly controlled and limited as to where they can actually hunt. Once they find an area with sufficient amounts of deer sign to hunt, they still need to locate a tree of a specific size in that area to safely support their treestand and body weight. Hopefully, one with enough branches and leaves or a tree large enough in diameter to hide their body from the deer's vision. And then this particular tree must be located close enough to the trail or the area where the deer are traveling to get a bow shot off at a deer. Treestands should not dictate where you are to hunt. The deer sign, the terrain, and the natural cover do that. You should only use treestands as tools to help you kill your deer—and use them only when all the conditions are right to use them. There will probably be more times and situations when you will not be able to use a treestand than there will be to use them. Natural ground blinds are sometimes more effective for ambushing deer than treestands.

One of the most controversial items of discussion among deer hunters today is the use of "buck lures" and if they really work. Well, this was one mystery that I personally wanted to investigate. I have tried using them in the past, and in most situations all they ever did was spook the deer. I did not know if I was using them incorrectly or using the wrong buck lure. I wanted to know, and the deer in my study areas were prime test animals to try them on. I knew that most of these deer had never, ever been hunted by humans. I knew that they had never been exposed to buck lures and I knew they would show me what I wanted to know.

Over a fifteen-year period I used and tested just about every buck lure sold to the hunting public. They were used before, during, and after the rut. They were used on hundreds of different wild whitetail deer of both sexes, of

Here's a good example of a territorial rub, and on a tree this size it's probably made by a big buck. Good place for a treestand? Maybe not; it depends on the wind conditions that made the buck use this area.

all ages, in many different study areas, and in various hunting areas of many different states. They were used in many different ways, and in many situations, and the deers' reactions were always observed from some distance away. I believe that the field tests of these buck lures were

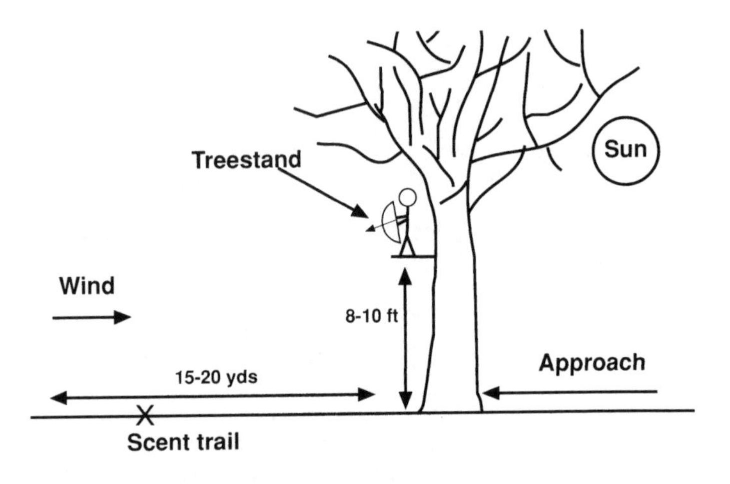

Place your stand with the wind to your front and the sun and some branches to your back. Use a direct approach into the wind.

fair and conclusive. The following is my opinion regarding many of the commercial buck lures on the market today. Since it's my opinion, you can take it or leave it!

Many of these so-called buck lures spooked the deer as soon as they passed within scenting distance of the sterile cotton balls with drops of buck lure on them. After sniffing some of these same buck lures myself, I could really understand why. To me, most of them just did not smell anything close to that of a deer's natural odor—and there is a good reason why.

Many of these products known as buck lures are collected from pen-raised deer. These penned-up deer could be whitetails, fallow deer, red deer, whatever. Regardless of their species, they are generally all penned up together in an area that has a wire mesh screen type of floor. Built underneath this wire floor there is usually some type of a collector pan with a built-in funnel that drains into another pan or into a bottle below. When these penned-up deer defecate and urinate, their excrements fall through the wire mesh floor into the collector pan and funnel, and then it flows down into the bottle. It is a great collection method, but the method of collection is not the problem, it is the contents.

These deer of various species have been raised on and are fed daily with livestock feed or other commercially produced food products. They do not eat the same natural foods that deer living in the wild eat, and the chemistry and odor of their excrements are going to be totally different from that of wild, free-ranging deer. Furthermore, the chemistry and the natural odor of the water that these penned deer drink are not the same as the water that is found in other regions of the country. The water found in Pennsylvania or Oregon tastes and smells much different and is chemically different from the water found in Virginia, North Carolina, or Montana. The urine produced by deer drinking water from one area is not going to be the same as the deer urine from another area. The chemistry of the urine is different and the odor of the urine is different.

Along with all the mixed species of deer urine, the fecal droppings, the dirt, the food, the rain, and anything else that falls or is windblown onto the mesh floor drains into the same collection bottle—not to mention any chemical or metal residues that flow into the bottle as the result of uric acids dripping through the metal flooring. This final mixture, derived from pen-raised deer, and whatever else that fell into the bottle, is what is sometimes strained, bottled, and sold to the general hunting public as "buck lure." Considering all these facts, you do not really need a degree in science to figure out why many of these products spook deer. They are not the real thing! They are chemically different. They smell different, and wild deer know it.

Some "buck lures" that I tested, the ones that smelled to me more like the natural odor of deer, did actually attract some young bucks to various test areas without spooking them. Many of these young bucks actually licked the cotton balls that had drops of these buck lures on them. However, these same tagged, young bucks would not return to the buck lure ever again. Most would just scent-check the area from a safe distance downwind and move away. Most of the does spooked and ran from the test areas as soon as they detected the scent of these buck lures in the air.

In many hunting situations, from Virginia to Quebec, the buck lures that seemed to work occasionally in my study areas spooked the deer that I was hunting. After many disappointing trips to the woods, I finally came to believe that the use of buck lures by thousands and thousands of desperate, sloppy, stinky deer hunters in the woods of the eastern United States over many past and current hunting seasons has conditioned the deer that these particular scents are that of man, and danger. This is why many deer spook and run when buck lure scents are present. Deer hunters of past and present have overused and misused these products for so long that they have actually taught the deer to fear them. The same way other deer hunters have taught the deer that bacon and eggs, coffee, etc., were the scents of man, and danger.

A few good buck lures may occasionally draw a young buck to a scented area—even a mature buck in a remote area that has seen very little hunting pressure. However, older, wiser deer that have survived one deer hunting season in heavily pressured country will usually spook and

Another good example of where the well-used scent trail, left, diverges from the territorial trail. Try to set up downwind of the scent trail, not on the territorial trail itself.

run whenever the scent of overused, man-made "buck lures" appears in the woods.

I believe very few of the many so-called buck lures on the market actually work. It is my opinion, especially in heavily pressured areas, that you are much better off going into woods without any scents whatsoever. All you are really doing using bad lures is letting the deer know that you, or that something strange, is in the woods. It defeats the whole idea of a perfect ambush!

I have developed my own "natural method" of luring whitetail bucks to me. Whenever legal, I kill a deer, buck, or doe near the time of the rut, or find a fresh road kill. I remove the deer's bladder, with urine, and cut off both musk glands and use them to lure deer to me. As I explained to you before, deer are herd animals and by being so, they generally seek out other deer for companionship and safety. By taking a dead deer's musk glands and urine and placing them in the woods, I am basically setting this same deer back in the woods without its body. Any deer moving through these woods downwind eventually scents this deer's musk and urine and it believes that another deer is somewhere upwind. Out of curiosity it naturally comes to see. Especially the mature, breeding bucks.

If a mature buck scents the musk glands and urine of another whitetail buck downwind close by his home range territory during the rut, he will more than likely come running to the area to drive the buck out of his mating territory, provided he is not currently paired up with a doe. If the buck scents a doe's musk glands and urine, especially if she was in estrous when she was killed, he will usually come trotting and grunting to the source of the scent, again provided the buck is not already paired up with another doe. This is why the sex of the dead deer that is used is not really important. It is the musk glands and urine that make it all happen. I learned this little trick a long time ago by observing the behavior of other deer walking up to many of the dead deer that I had killed in the past. They came unalarmed and sniffed at the musk glands of the dead deer still lying on the ground. Usually, after a few moments of sniffing, they just slowly walked away, even though sometimes blood was present on the ground.

CHAPTER TEN

USING NATURAL LURES; THE "STALKING STICK"

My method of luring mature, trophy-class whitetail bucks has worked for me many times in heavily hunted public hunting areas throughout the eastern United States. However, it does require meticulous care and handling of the musk glands and urine to be successful.

As I mentioned before, you need the musk glands and the urine off of a recently killed deer. If they happen to come off a doe that was in estrous, so much the better. Cut the musk glands off both hind legs and cut or punch a small hole in one end of each one. Then tie a washed out, air-dried piece of string about 18 inches long to each one and put each musk gland in separate, washed out, resealable plastic sandwich bags. Use the plastic bags to carry the musk glands home for storage or to where you plan to use them. Before you put the glands into the plastic bags, take a real good sniff of them and you will learn, and know, the "real scent" of whitetail deer. Try not to handle or touch the musk glands too much while you are cutting them off or attaching the string to them. You do not want to taint them with human scent or deer could be spooked by them. Do not use any glands that have spoiled or that have or had any blood on them or they will spook the deer. You can store them, sealed up in the plastic bags, in a refrigerator for four to seven days before the musk glands will begin to lose the potency of their scent. Then they should be replaced with fresh ones.

To remove the deer's bladder and the urine contained inside, you should use a small pair of pruning shears to cut through each side of the pelvis bone which covers and protects the bladder. Many hunters just chop through the pelvis bone with their hunting knives when they quickly field dress their deer. However, many times they also chop or cut into the deer's bladder or the bladder is punctured by bone fragments and the urine spills out into the pelvic cavity and, most times, on some areas of exposed meat. Small pruning shears make removal of the deer's pelvic bone and bladder very quick and easy, without spilling the urine and tainting the meat. You may need to use your knife, just a little, to cut away any flesh that sometimes clings to the pelvis bone to make its removal a little easier.

After you have removed the pelvic bone, tie off the urethral end of the bladder with a small piece of string to prevent the urine from leaking out—much the way a surgeon would tie off a bleeding artery or vein. You do not have to tie off the two very small ureters, the vessels connecting the deer's kidneys to the bladder, as they are so small that very little urine will leak out of them. Now, cut through the urethra above the tied string, and gently lift the bladder up out of its cavity and put it into a washed out, resealable plastic sandwich bag for storage until you get home. Then empty the contents of the bladder into a couple of small, sterile, watertight plastic bottles. You can freeze or keep the urine in a cool place until you need to use it, but do not freeze the musk glands or they will lose their potency. Musk glands need to be somewhat fresh to really work well.

To best use the glands and urine, locate yourself

somewhere in the bottomlands of the herd's home range territory where you can best use the wind to your advantage to carry the "musk and urine" scent as far downwind as possible. You want any deer that passes downwind at any distance to pick up the scent. When you decide exactly where you are going to hunt, open the bottles of urine and pour enough urine into each plastic bag containing the musk glands so that each gland, with its string still attached, is completely soaked with urine. Using the string only, take one of the musk glands out of its plastic bag and walk fifteen to twenty yards out to the left of where you plan to sit while you are hunting. Then turn and walk upwind another fifteen to twenty yards above where you plan to sit. Now, take the urine-soaked musk gland and holding the string, swing it around up over your head a few times, as a cowboy would swing a lariat. Then tie the end of the string to a low tree branch or anything else that would allow the musk gland to hang free in the wind twelve to sixteen inches off the ground. Now, take the other musk gland out of the plastic bag by the string, and walk fifteen to twenty yards out to the right of where you are going to sit. Then turn and walk upwind the same distance and swing that urine soaked gland around up over your head a few times and hang it in the same manner as you did the first.

The purpose of swinging the urine-soaked musk glands around up over your head is to spray droplets of deer urine mixed with "musk scent" all over the area that you are hunting, and on you. This floods an area of woods with a lot of fresh deer scent and any deer that passes this scent anywhere downwind is tricked into believing that there is one or more deer in that area. The spray of a little deer urine on you and your clothes provides you with a real good cover scent in this particular situation. When the deer come to investigate all this fresh deer scent they will be coming unalarmed, with their noses into the wind. Since most of the "musk and urine" scent, and the strongest source of the scent, is placed out to the sides and farther upwind behind you, the deer will not suspect any danger as they approach the area and pass by you. The perfect ambush!

Once again, if you use this method and you lure a young buck or a doe into shooting range, the musk glands and urine have done their job. If you do not kill that young deer, you are not doing your job. All you will be doing is teaching that deer to avoid that scent in the future. If that young buck, or doe, happens to circle the "scented area" downwind after it discovers that there is no other deer around and it picks up your scent downwind, it will remember and avoid your scent as well for as long as it lives, and it will look for you whenever it passes through that section of woods again.

If you are a trophy hunter only and you are real clean and quiet, this musk gland and urine setup could work for you all day long and it will usually attract many deer to the area. Most of the deer that are drawn to this "scented area" will usually just wander off after a while, sometimes slightly confused, yet unalarmed, searching for the deer that left all the scent in the area. Many times some of the bucks that are drawn to the "scented area" will make a ground scrape, or they will feed around the area until they are driven away by larger, more mature bucks as they arrive. Other times, the deer may become very anxious or curious and they will continuously circle downwind of the area, constantly scent-checking for any out-of-place odor in the air or on the ground. Especially if a deer happened to walk right into one of the musk

One of many bucks the author has lured with his "musk glands and urine" setup during the rut. This big buck weighed in at 207 pounds.

glands that were hanging from a low branch with its nose. If you should kill a deer in the "scented area" or your scent is picked up downwind by a deer intent on finding you and it spooks and blows a warning to other deer, immediately take your musk glands and leave the woods. Your hunting is over in that area of the woods for the day. Otherwise, you will be just teaching all the deer in the area your scent and how you hunt.

Antler rattling, grunt calls, etc., all fall into the same category as buck lures, as far as I am concerned. I don't use these techniques in the country I hunt and have no confidence in them. However, in fairness, I have spent very little energy on testing these methods and devices. I would never say that these attempts to attract whitetail bucks never work. Some of these things may work on some deer under the right conditions. However, as more and more deer hunters use antler rattling, grunt calls, doe

This huge-bodied P&Y buck is the one that was fooled by a bag of dirty clothes left on a portable treestand. While he was scent-checking the author's laundry he was arrowed from a downwind ambush site.

bleats, etc., it will be only a matter of time before most all the deer in the eastern United States learn to spook and run from them.

I have tried antler rattling in combination with my musk glands and urine four to five times and, on one occasion I did lure a mature whitetail buck—which is actually a pretty good average! However, I do not know for sure what attracted him—the "musk and urine" scent, or the rattling of antlers. I have lured many trophy, class whitetail bucks using just musk glands and urine alone and I have watched many other bucks, both young and old, run from the noise of rattling antlers.

On another occasion I tried to rattle in a very large whitetail buck after he approached a "scented area" in a very thick, bottomland section of the woods along the

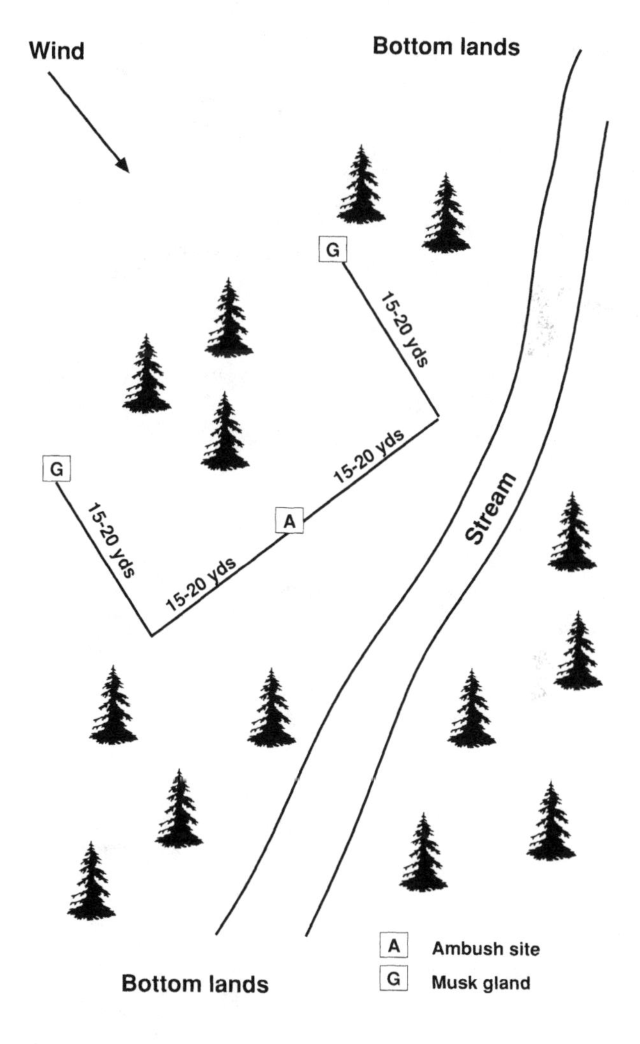

Use of scent glands as both *lure* and *cover scent*.

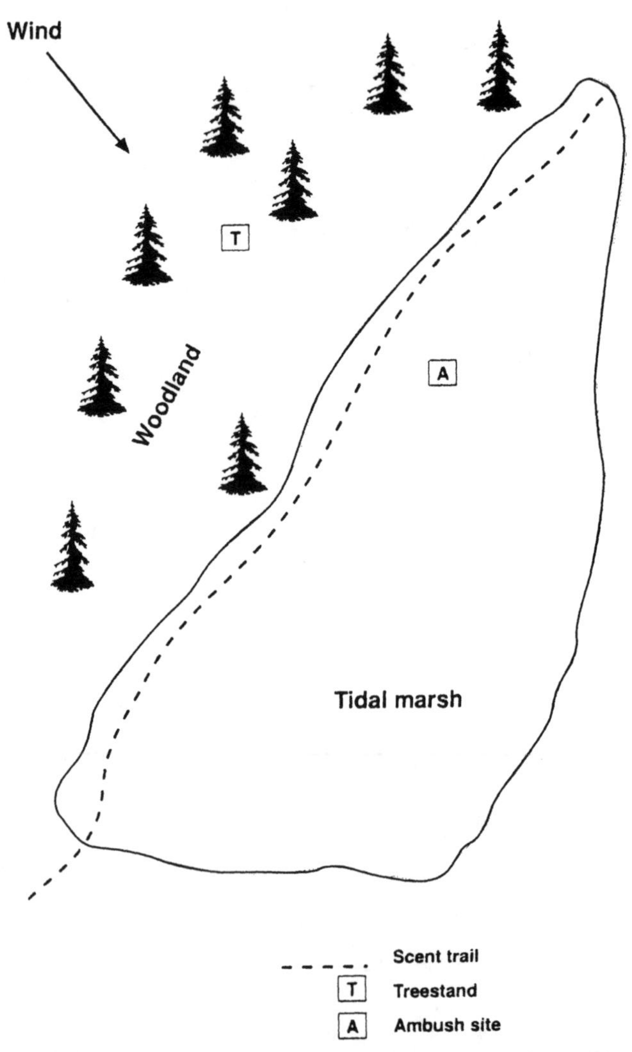

I put dirty clothes in the treestand knowing the buck would scent-check it . . . then put my ambush site fifteen yards downwind!

edge of a river's tidal marsh. The buck passed me at twenty to twenty-five yards, out away from me, at a fast trot through a very dense thicket that I could not shoot an arrow through. After finding no deer in the "scented area," the buck made a scrape on the ground, then became very curious and slowly began to circle out around, downwind of the scent. Before he could get directly downwind of me, I rattled the antlers enough to get his attention, and watched him disappear in the distance. From some distance downwind the buck eventually picked up my scent, let out a blow and took off.

I hunted for that buck four or five other days during the rut when the winds were right for him to be moving through that area again. Each time, from a different location, I could see him scent-checking the air for me as he traveled through a tidal marsh 50 to 60 yards downwind of me. The buck knew my scent and he knew every time that I was in the woods thanks to antler rattling. I killed this buck a week later while I was standing in tall marsh-grass up to my knees in mud and water, as the buck passed downwind of my portable treestand looking for me. While the buck was scent-checking a bag of my dirty hunting clothes that I had purposely left on my treestand that morning for him to scent—to trick him—I shot an arrow through his liver from my position in the marsh fifteen yards downwind of his scent trail. This fine buck dressed out at 219 pounds and he carried an eight-point set of antlers that scored 127 3/8 P&Y. It is my firm opinion that you should enter, hunt, and leave the woods with the least possible disturbance and not allow the deer to learn your scent, or how or where you hunt. I believe that deer hunters should carry as little scent as possible into the woods, and make as little noise as possible. It works for me!

The major problem for most hunters is walking in the woods. Especially when the leaves on the ground are dry, and they sound like you are smashing corn flakes whenever you step on them. All animals in the woods make noise when they walk through dry leaves. Deer and other animals in the woods are not necessarily spooked by the noisy crunching of leaves; they are used to it. They *are* spooked by the uncommon rhythm and sound of a human's walk in the woods. It sounds different, it is out of place, and it really stands out. Sounds carry a long distance in the woods and most all the animals know when a human is traveling through. They can hear the sound of a human's walking rhythm from hundreds of yards away. I can hear the difference 100 yards away myself, depending on conditions.

All animals in the woods walk on four legs and when they walk they always have two legs moving, which produces a certain rhythm and sound to their movement. Humans have two legs and when they walk they only have one leg moving at any given time, and no matter how slow a human walks, his walking rhythm always sounds the same. A human's walking rhythm sounds like a steady "cheh, cheh, cheh, cheh, cheh," while a deer's walking rhythm sounds more like "cheh cheh, cheh cheh, cheh cheh, cheh cheh."

I use a "stalking stick" whenever I still-hunt or travel through the woods, or stalk in for a close bow shot at a deer, a bear, etc. The stalking stick functions as my "third leg" and it helps me produce the same walking rhythm and sound of a deer or another large animal walking in the woods. The stalking stick that I most commonly use is an old shovel handle, painted a dark color and cut to a length so that it is no taller than the bottom of my rib cage, with the thickest end of the handle used on the

A "stalking stick" enables you to mimic a deer's rhythm as you still-hunt or stalk through dry leaves in the woods. It takes just a bit of practice to get the cadence right.

ground. Many times, as I enter the woods to hunt I will just pick up a solid, dead branch that is lying on the ground and break it to the length that I need and use it as my stalking stick. The size and weight are somewhat critical. It needs to be at least the same size and diameter of a deer's lower front leg in order to produce a noise that sounds similar to what a deer's leg produces, and heavy enough to blend in with the sounds of your feet when you are moving.

There is a proper way to walk in the woods and there is a proper way to use a stalking stick. Nothing in the woods moves fast unless it has been disturbed. If you move too fast, your movements and sounds will spook the birds, squirrels, etc., and their spooked movements and calls will alert the deer and other animals in the woods and they will know that something is wrong. It is very important that you move just as slow as a deer normally walks when it is feeding. When you walk on dry leaves and use a stalking stick, walk more on the balls of your feet and scuff your feet along the ground. Take short, choppy steps, and push your feet through and under the leaves as you walk, rather than stepping down flat-footed on the leaves.

Deer and other animals naturally walk with their front feet pushing through the leaves. They do not step down on top of them. The joint where the deer's hoof is connected to the front leg bends backward as they lift their hoof from the ground. As a deer's front leg is moved forward again, the hoof is sort of snapped or slung forward, which naturally propels the hoof to slide through and under the leaves as they walk. The rear hooves of deer also slide through and under the leaves when they walk. A human's foot and ankle joint works just the opposite and that is why you should scuff your feet through the leaves when you walk. Scuffing produces the same action sounds a deer's hooves make.

To best use the stalking stick, hold it in your free hand and grip it like you would a ski pole with your forearm parallel to the ground and the stalking stick angling back toward the heel of your foot. As you walk and scuff your

There was no telephoto lens in this photo. This big-bodied, large-racked mature buck was stalked within 30 yards using a stalking stick.

feet, lift the stalking stick off the ground, and with a little wrist action snap the bottom of the stalking stick forward and down at the same time into the leaves, imitating the deer's front leg movement. The stalking stick should be used in between every step you take with your feet to simulate the deer's other legs moving, which produces the "cheh cheh, cheh cheh" effect when you walk. Try to imagine what a deer or other four-legged animal sounds like when they walk in dry leaves and mimic their rhythm. You can practice this in the woods near your house. It does not really take a whole lot of effort, but you do need to perfect the rhythm and sound of a deer walking. Ask a friend or neighbor to work with you while you practice. Close your eyes and listen to your friend walk through the leaves as a human, then with the stalking stick and hear the difference.

When you walk in dry, noisy woods, take no more than ten steps or so without stopping for at least five to ten seconds. This simulates a deer moving and browsing and it will not spook the deer, the birds, or any other animals in the woods. No animal in the woods moves continuously without stopping unless there is danger, except predators. Use a stalking stick whenever you still-hunt or travel through the woods. Move and walk through the woods slowly, constantly scanning all around you, looking for movement or for any horizontal figures in the woods. Most everything in the woods grows vertically and most all horizontal things will stand out to your vision. Most horizontal things in the woods are either logs, deer, or other animals.

Do not watch the ground too much as you walk or you may miss out on everything else that is happening up ahead of you or around you. Just look quickly ahead on the ground, 20 yards or so, to see what you will be walking through or over. Then watch for movement deeper in the woods as you slowly move toward the end of the 20-yard distance you just scanned. Repeat this same process of movement over and over as you walk through the woods hunting. This is basically what still-hunting is. It is a simple, very effective way to hunt any game and the best way to approach your treestand area. Just keep the wind always blowing in your face as you move, so the wind does not blow your scent far ahead of you and alert the deer or other animals of your approach. Watch for movement and use the stalking stick.

Most of the photographs of big bucks and other deer shown in this book were taken after I stalked into them with a stalking stick. Most all of the deer that I have killed while they were sleeping in their beds were fooled by the stalking stick.

CHAPTER ELEVEN

NIGHT VISION; BLOODTRAILING

When you enter the woods in the dark of morning, act and move as though you know deer are present in those woods and do not use a flashlight. Deer don't use them and beams of light shining off through the woods spook the deer and other animals. Use your own natural night vision! You can see very well in the dark, once the pupils of your eyes adjust to the darkness, especially on clear nights with bright stars or moonlight shining down on the land. You cannot read a map with night vision, or see the fine details of things, but you can see where you are walking and the shapes of objects and trees in the woods. You can see dead branches and logs lying on the ground, tree stumps, etc., and it is possible to see a deer moving through the woods twenty-five to fifty yards away. You may not be able to tell if it has a rack or not, but you could see that it is a deer. You see what a deer normally sees, with everything in shades of black and gray. Deer are colorblind.

It takes about 10 to 15 minutes for your eyes to become totally adjusted to the dark after looking at any artificial light source. Once your eyes have adjusted to the dark don't look at any artificial light source even for a split second, or the pupils of your eyes will react to the light and you will instantly lose your night vision. It will take another ten to fifteen minutes for your eyes to adjust back to the darkness.

Try this little night vision experiment one night and you will see what I mean. Sometime before sundown go to the woods, or to an area where there is no artificial lighting, and wait for nightfall. Take a cigarette lighter or a small flashlight with you, but do not use them or look at any other artificial lights. Once darkness sets in your eyes will naturally adjust. Walk through the woods for a while and look at things out and around you, and you will see how amazingly well your eyes function in the dark. Now, close one eye and keep it closed. With one eye open, turn on the flashlight or cigarette lighter for a second or so, then turn it off and open your closed eye. Now you will see nothing but darkness out of the eye that was exposed to the artificial light. You will still have some partial night vision from the eye that you kept closed and you will be able to walk around and see things without tripping over them, but not as well as before your open eye saw the artificial light. Let your eyes adjust back to the darkness and once you are sure you have total night vision again, with both eyes open, turn on the flashlight or cigarette lighter for a second or so then turn it off. Now you will see nothing but pure darkness. Your night vision is gone and it will not be back until your eyes adjust to the dark again.

When you use night vision to enter or leave the woods during darkness, do not stare directly at any object off in the distance to determine what it is; just scan your eyes in small circles all around the object and you will see the shape of the object. Most all things in the woods during darkness will generally appear to you as black objects. If you stare at a black object your eyes will tend to focus in on the black area of the object and you lose its shape. If you scan your vision all around the object, your eyes will

The buzzards are out there waiting for deer shot by hunters lacking the experience, common sense, and patience to bloodtrail properly!

pick up all the available light around the outline of the black object, and you will be able to see its shape in the darkness.

If you have to cross a large, open area before you enter the woods during darkness, you should stop just inside the woods for a few minutes to allow your eyes to adjust to the darker woods. Open areas are normally much brighter than the woods, and it will take a couple of minutes for your eyes to totally adjust to the darker area.

I learned about night vision in the military in jungle warfare training and I used it daily in the jungles of Vietnam. I was a point man and scout in a Recon unit. I used night vision on nighttime ambush and Recon patrols and I use night vision to enter and leave the woods wherever I hunt. Night vision works! Use it and save your flashlight for an emergency or for following a blood trail at night. If you feel you must use a flashlight to enter or leave the woods during darkness, use one that has a red, nighttime lens. It will allow you to see where you are walking without sending beams of bright light shining off through the woods and it is less likely to spook the deer in other nearby areas. However, the red glow of the flashlight may spook the deer in the area of woods where you are walking.

Whenever possible never walk across or along the edge of open crop fields or pastures. Some of the best browsing foods grow along the edge of the fields and woods and deer frequently bed and feed along the edges of open fields during the night. Deer have much larger eyes than humans and they have much better night vision. They will definitely see you coming from great distances away, and the deer will scent or hear you should you approach the woods with the wind quartering or coming off your back. Use night vision and a stalking stick and circle out around the area you plan to hunt, until you can walk to that area with the wind in your face. This simple step alone could make a big difference in how many deer you may see in a morning's hunt. At least you won't be driving the deer out of the fields and into the woods spooked to warn any other deer in the area.

When you bowhunt for deer, you should always shoot the first deer that comes within your shooting range, and you should always take the first opportune shot at that deer. Too many hunters wait for the "perfect bowshot" and wind up with no shot at all, or they wound the deer because they rushed off a last-minute shot at the deer. Any deer that you kill with a bow is a trophy, and unless you have taken a lot of deer with the bow, you need the experience to prepare you for trophy bowhunting. Besides, if you can only hunt on weekends, you may not see another deer

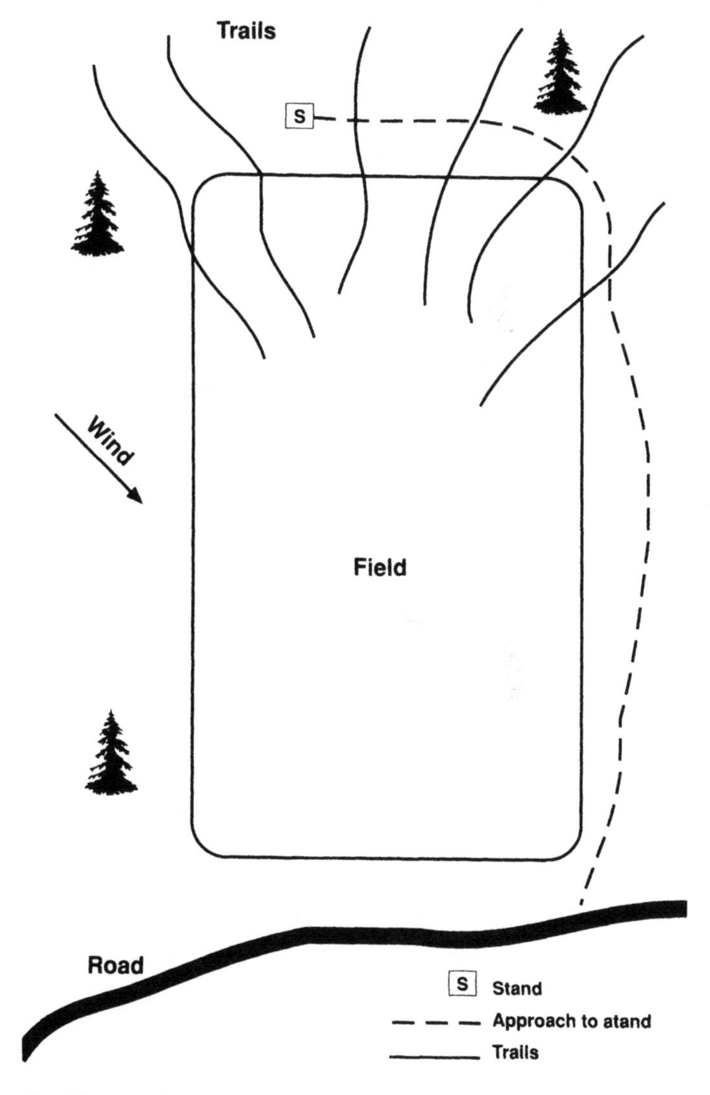

Avoid open fields and edges when approaching a stand in the dark; the deer will surely see you!

or have the opportunity to kill a deer at close range for the rest of the bowhunting season. You need to get some experience killing deer. The more deer you take with the bow, the more settled your mind becomes when deer are at short distances from you. The more deer you kill, the more experienced you will become in bloodtrailing, tracking, etc. If you do not learn these things, sooner or later you may get a chance to kill a trophy buck and you may wound that buck and lose his blood trail, simply because you lack the experience to read and understand the blood evidence and tracks.

Bowhunting is like any other profession or trade; you need the exposure and the experience to become good at it. Welders usually do not start out welding the watertight seams on the hulls of nuclear submarines when they first learn how to weld and doctors do not begin to practice medicine the same day they graduate from medical school. They all go through years of training before they ever get their journeyman rating or license to practice their profession or trade, and the same laws of experience apply to bowhunting. Each deer that you kill with the bow will teach you a different lesson. You learn and understand why, and how far, wounded deer travel after being shot by an arrow through different vital areas and various other wounds, and the difference in their blood trails.

You will learn that a deer that has been shot high, through both lungs, usually only leaves scattered drops of blood on the ground as it blindly runs away in panic during the first forty to sixty yards until the lungs fill up with blood to the level of the arrow holes. Then the blood pours out the arrow holes and leaves a solid blood trail on the ground to follow. Many deer that are shot high through the lungs are lost by hunters because they cannot find enough blood or tracks on the ground during the first twenty to 30

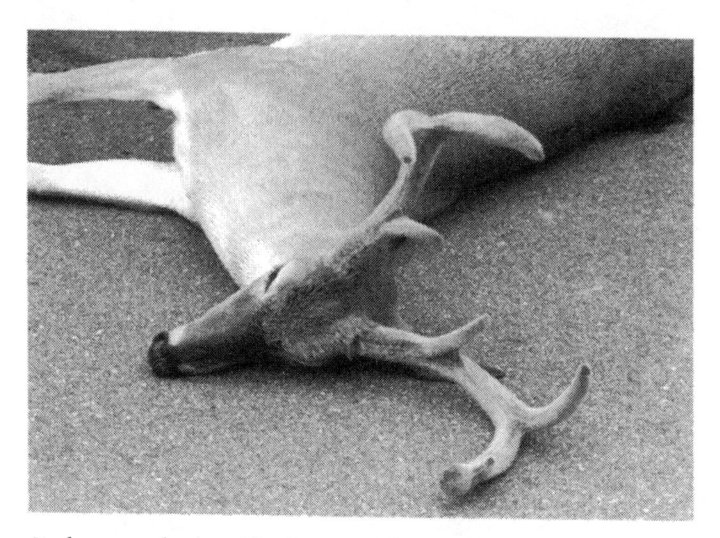

Early-season bucks—like this one with summer coat and antlers still in velvet—can easily be lost to heat and blowflies. Good tracking skills are even more critical then.

yards of their bloodtrailing to find the trail of the wounded deer. Especially a deer that has been shot high through only one of its lungs. Then the blood trail usually starts out with only a few small drops of blood on the ground, four to six feet apart for the first 20 to 80 yards, until the damaged lung fills up with blood to the arrow hole. Then the blood pours out of the wound and leaves a heavy blood trail on the ground to follow. A deer that has been shot through only one of its lungs usually travels 120 to 200 yards before the damaged lung fills up with blood and the other lung collapses, causing death.

You will learn that a deer that has been shot through the low lung area usually leaves a heavy blood trail on the ground within the first few yards from where they were shot and that they usually die within forty to eighty yards. The blood trail of a deer that has been shot through the lung area usually contains many tiny air bubbles in the blood. This is caused by the mixing of air sucked in through the arrow holes with the blood from within the damaged lungs.

You will learn that a deer that has been shot through the heart or liver usually travels less than forty yards and it leaves a heavy blood trail from the spot where it was shot. Many hunters try for heart shots on deer for quicker kills. However, most fail to realize that a liver shot is just as fatal as a heart shot. The liver is five to six times larger than the heart and much easier to hit with an arrow. The liver filters all the blood that flows through the deer's body and it always contains several times the volume of blood found in a deer's heart. An arrow through the liver on any animal causes massive bleeding and a very quick death.

A deer that has been shot in the spine or backbone, behind the shoulders, is instantly paralyzed and loses all functions of its rear legs. It may try to pull itself along the ground with its front legs, but it will not travel very far. A deer that has been shot in the neck vertebrae loses movement of all four legs. These types of wounds are not instantly fatal. They only immobilize the deer and a second arrow should be shot quickly through the deer's heart or liver to hasten its death.

A deer that has been shot through a major body muscle usually leaves a blood trail with signs of heavy bleeding during the first thirty to sixty yards. Then the blood trail slowly diminishes to small puddles, or large drops of blood every ten to twelve feet over the next eighty to 100 yards. Eventually there's nothing at all, except the deer's tracks. These muscle, or meat wounds, are not usually fatal to deer. Most times the deer that have been wounded in this fashion will usually drink lots of water and they will purposely lie down on their bleeding wounds to try to stop the bleeding. Deer have a most special blood running through their arteries and veins. It has a very high coagulation rate and when direct pressure is applied to an open wound or damaged blood vessels, the blood clots very fast and prevents any further loss. When a deer is wounded and it loses a lot of blood, its tongue and its mouth becomes very dry and this naturally compels the deer to find water to quench its thirst. When the deer drinks, precious lost liquids are quickly replenished in the deer's circulatory system, blood pressure is raised and after a few hours of rest the deer is well on its way to a speedy recovery.

A deer that has been shot through the stomach or the intestines, called gutshot or paunched, usually leaves a very faint blood trail on the ground, consisting of a few small drops of blood or intestinal fluid four to six feet apart, for sometimes hundreds of yards. It is very important that you begin tracking a gutshot deer soon after the deer has left your eyesight or you will probably lose that deer. Many of these so-called "bow hunting instructors" tell you to wait an hour or so before you start bloodtrailing a gutshot deer. This is because most of these people have not killed, wounded, bloodtrailed, or tracked enough deer to know any better. If you wait ten minutes that is long enough. The longer you wait, the harder it is going to be to find a gutshot deer's blood trail and tracks. Especially if the deer is only dropping intestinal fluid on the ground occasionally.

When a deer is gutshot, the stomach muscles are usually cut and damaged enough to cause that deer to slightly drag its hind feet as it runs or walks away. The cut stomach muscles usually prevent the wounded deer from fully stretching out its front and hind legs, so the deer's hind feet are more pulled forward and dragged, rather than lifted, leaving drag marks on the ground. Many times these drag marks and the dark underneath sides of leaves kicked up

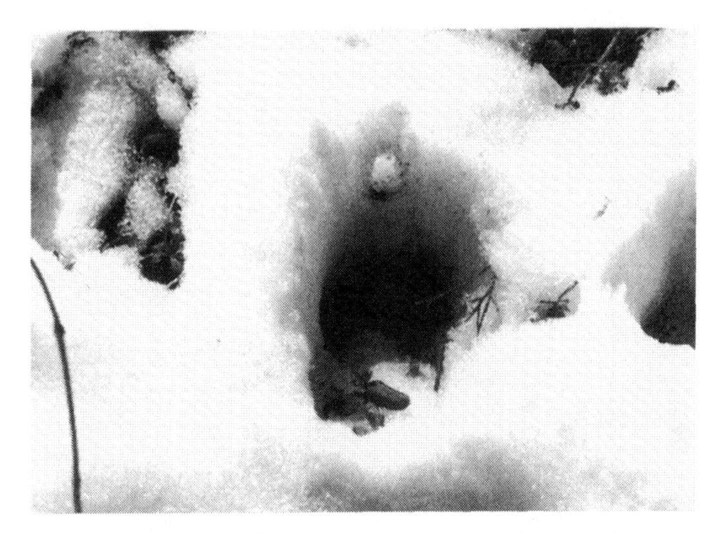

Tracking and bloodtrailing are greatly simplified by snow, but even without it the evidence is usually there to follow if you think and take your time.

by the gutshot deer as it slightly drags its hind feet, plus occasional drops of blood or intestinal fluid, are all there is for you to follow. If you do not move quickly to follow this fresh sign, the sun, the wind, or other climatic conditions will quickly destroy them and you will probably never find that deer.

A gutshot deer will usually travel 150 to 300 yards with the wind to its back to be sure nothing is following it. Then it will usually circle back around its trail a short distance and lie down with the wind to its back twenty to thirty yards off its original trail and watch its backtrack for anything that may follow. A gutshot deer usually dies a slow death wherever it first lies down unless it is pressured to move. The whole purpose of bloodtrailing and tracking a gutshot deer as soon as possible after it is shot is to pressure the wounded deer to keep moving, so you can find it.

Every time it jumps up and moves it loses a little more blood or intestinal fluid, a little more life energy, and it leaves more fresh sign on the ground for you to follow. Eventually, a gutshot deer will run out of energy and become too weak to move and it will lie down one last time. You may have to kill this deer with a quick shot to the heart or liver when you come up on it, if it has not already expired. But at least you will be able to recover the gutshot deer and the meat from the woods before the turkey buzzards find it.

The more deer you kill, wound, and blood trail, the better you will become at bloodtrailing and tracking. And, when you have taken a lot of deer with the bow, you will naturally become a selective trophy hunter. Not that many people consistently kill trophy bucks with a bow year after year unless they really know and understand deer behavior and know the land they hunt on very well. Learn your lessons well!

CHAPTER TWELVE

TIMING THE HUNT; SHOOTING TIPS

One key to success in hunting deer is to hunt in areas where there are large numbers of deer. If you do not know of any such areas, check with your state's wildlife management department and find out where the largest populations of deer are located. Most states perform some type of yearly census survey on the deer populations in different areas of the state and they usually know where large numbers of deer are located. Most states are quite helpful and they will usually send you state game bulletins and maps of various wildlife management areas that have large deer populations. Travel to one of those areas during the late winter to scout for enough deer sign to warrant your hunting there and to learn the territory.

Late winter is one of the best times of the year to scout for deer sign, especially right after a light rain- or snowstorm ends. At this time of the year the deer are still traveling through the same sections of their home range areas and herd's home range territory as they did in the early fall. The prevailing northerly winds control where the deer live and travel from early fall to late winter, and the prevailing southerly winds control their lives from early spring to early fall. Any frequently used deer trails, rubs or scrapes, scent trails, etc., you find in the woods during late winter will generally be used again by the same deer during next fall's rut. The tracks and other signs of individual bucks or other deer that lived past the last hunting season will show you where you should begin hunting for them when the time is right again.

Another good time to scout for deer sign and to hunt deer is right after the rise of the full moon in early October. As the moon nears its descending, three-quarter phase, most of the mature does of the herd will have experienced their first very short estrous cycle of the year, and the mature bucks will have already begun to extensively mark out their home range area along their territorial trails. You want to learn how the deer are traveling through the area, and the only way to do that is to find some fresh deer tracks and follow them to see where they lead. Still-hunt and scout for deer sign as you make your way through the woods until you either kill a deer or you find the perfect spot to ambush the deer.

Many times the winds at this time of the year are still primarily coming out of the south, and they are just beginning to shift out of the north occasionally. Any fresh rubs and scrapes or other deer sign you find during these periods of southerly winds should be noted and remembered well. Over many of the past years the doe's second heat cycle and the rut in early to mid-November have occurred during southerly winds and warm weather. Your knowledge of the deer herd's travel under southerly winds, should the winds shift from a northerly direction to southerly flow near the time for the rut, would show you where you should be hunting any time the winds are out of the south.

The best time of year to bowhunt for trophy deer in the woods is when most of the leaves have changed their colors and begin falling off the trees. This allows you to have a better vision of the open woods all around you when you hunt. You can hear or see deer traveling in the woods many yards away, and the deer sign is much more obvious and meaningful. Many times anxious bowhunters will take to the woods too early in the season, when the weather is too warm and before the leaves drop, and they miss out by not seeing what is happening in the woods all around them. A large buck or other deer could pass by thirty to forty feet away, and they would never know it because of the leaves on the trees blocking their view. Most of the deer seen or killed by early-season bowhunters are usually young deer, a year and a half old, or younger. The meat of many deer killed in the early bowseason, when the weather is too warm, is ruined by blowflies depositing maggot eggs or spoiled by the heat before the hunters can even get them out of the woods to the butcher or freezer. These early-season bow hunters also teach the deer of their scents and hunting habits and the older deer will know whenever they are in the woods again. Too much early-season hunting and scouting in any one area of the herd's home range territory may cause the deer to shift their daily travels over to new trail systems farther downwind.

You should not hunt from treestands on days of strong, gusty winds, unless you are hunting near a cover area, or you are just wasting your time. The deer will not be traveling around too much, or too far from their bedding areas, until the winds settle down somewhat. I have seen deer, moose, etc., bed down and stay in heavy cover for three days at a time during periods of strong rain or wind storms. However, after three days, most any animal will temporarily leave their cover area for other foods and water.

You should take advantage of the noisy conditions in the woods during strong windstorms to still-hunt the bedding and cover areas and to scout around the area you are hunting. The deer will not usually hear you moving around through the woods if you move slowly and use a stalking stick and you may get in close enough to get a shot off at a bedded deer. At least if you jump some deer up from their beds while you are still-hunting, you will learn where they will be bedding on these types of days in the future. Just remember where they were bedded and the wind and the weather conditions. Whenever those same conditions occur again, you will find them bedding down there again.

If you happen to stalk in to within fifteen yards or less of a deer or any other big game animal and the deer suddenly looks directly at you but it does not instantly spook and run away, quickly close one of your eyes. The deer may have heard or saw you moving, but it apparently does not know what you are. If your face and hands are totally camouflaged and you remain very still, the alerted deer will not usually spook and run until it hears or sees you moving again or it sees your eyes. Animal and human eyes tend to shine or glow and when you are very close to a deer they can see your two eyes shining out at them. Deer and other animals will focus in on and stare directly at your eyes, especially if you tend to blink your eyes too much. However, if you close one of your eyes while the deer is looking at you, it will not be able to see two shining objects looking directly at it and most times it will settle down and lose interest in you. Most natural predators have different colored lines of fur, or darkened areas, around their eyes or head areas to camouflage or hide their eyes from their prey!

Many times you can kill an alert deer while it is looking directly at you by slowly moving the upper limb of your bow in front of one of your eyes as you slowly raise your bow up and pull your arrow back to full draw at the same time. Most deer will shift their heads slightly as they watch your very slow movements, but they usually will not spook

The author believes the instinctive method of shooting the bow is best for bowhunting, allowing quick, accurate bow shots even at moving targets.

and run until after the arrow touches them, unless you move too fast or wait too long to release your arrow. Should the deer spook and run as you slowly raise your bow and draw your arrow, you can still make a vital shot on that deer while it is running way from you, by sending an arrow right into the center of the bobbing, white rump area. The arrow will usually pass completely through the intestines and through most of the vital organs with very little resistance to the flight of the arrow, as the broadhead cuts through the body toward or out the chest. This is one vital shot at a running deer that most bowhunters totally overlook. Most deer shot this way travel less than forty yards, if that.

I have shot many deer that were running away from me this way after they jumped up from their beds, and I highly recommend this bow shot for anyone who is a quick, accurate, instinctive shooter. However, I do not suggest that a slow shooting, five pin, fixed sight bowhunter using a mechanical release ever try this bow shot because there would usually not be enough time for them to get prepared to shoot. I have been an "instinctive" bow shooter since I was eleven years old. I have never used sights on my bow and I have killed many large and small game animals while they were running away from me. I have also killed just as many ducks, geese, grouse, pheasants, wild turkeys, etc., while they were running or flying away from me. I have been a state champion–quality archer for many years, competing in organized archery as an "instinctive bowhunter," and I firmly believe that the instinctive method of shooting the bow and arrow is the best way to hunt animals in the woods.

For those of you that use or need to use sight pins on your bow when you hunt, I highly recommend that you use only one sight pin, set at twenty-five yards, for all your shooting, hunting, and practice. With the very flat trajectory of arrows coming off the "state-of-the-art" compound and recurve bows of today, the arrow flight rises and drops very little from zero to forty yards. One sight pin, set at twenty-five yards, would enable most any archer to accurately hit a small target area, or the center of a deer's vital organs, at forty yards, easily with a little practice. For example, if one sight pin was set at twenty-five yards on an average sixty-pound bow, a bowhunter would only need to raise the pin from the centerline of the deer's chest to the top of its back to place an arrow in the center of a deer's chest and vital organs at forty yards. If a deer was only ten yards away, the bowhunter would only need to drop the pin two to three inches, if that, below the centerline of the deer's chest, to place the arrow in the center of the deer's chest.

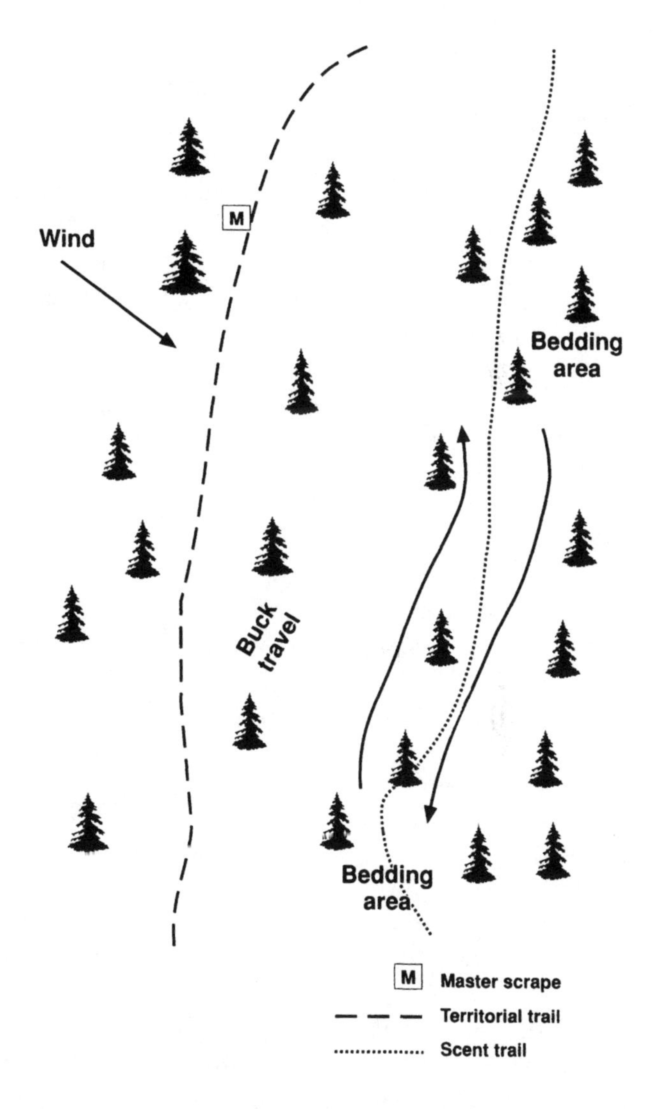

In midday hours during the rut bucks will travel back and forth between bedding areas, *scent-checking* the *master scrape.*

This is a very fast, accurate way for any bowhunter who uses sights on his bow to shoot quickly at running or flying game, especially if the bowhunter shoots the bow from a high anchor position and off the fingers, rather than a mechanical release. This shooting method totally eliminates the decision of what sight pin to use for what yardage, lining up peep sights, etc. The rise and fall of the arrow flight trajectory will vary from bow to bow and person to person, and should be determined while you are setting up your bow, setting your one sight pin, and during lots of practice.

I have taught "instinctive" and "one sight pin" bow shooting to hundreds of bowhunters over the past years, specifically for shooting at big game forty yards and under. I firmly believe that if you cannot accurately shoot an arrow at forty yards, a mere 120 feet, you do not belong in the woods with a bow in your hand. Too many times you will see deer or other big game animals traveling thirty to forty yards away from you and you should be able to kill them. This "forty-yard" shooting distance is only a limitation of your mind and lack of practice, and not of the bow!

You should not hunt from treestands on rainy days, or not at all during rainy days in my opinion. Once again, the deer are going to be bedded down in heavy cover, and they will not travel around too much until the rain slows down to a drizzle or stops. I have seen deer traveling around during periods of light rain and you are always going to hear of some hunter who, by pure luck, took a nice buck while hunting in the rain. But, the odds are really against you. Your hunting clothes are going to get soaking wet. Wet clothes stink and the deer will definitely scent them and you, too. If you should happen to wound a deer on a rainy day, you will probably lose that deer. It is pretty hard to follow a blood trail that is being washed away as quickly as the rain falls, and the odds of finding a wounded or dead

This huge-bodied buck was taken at forty-five yards while standing and feeding in a honeysuckle thicket during the rut. He dressed out at 214 pounds.

deer the next day, or after the rain ends, is about as good as a blind man bowhunting pheasants! In all my years of bowhunting, and all the animals that I have killed with arrows, I have lost to the woods and buzzards only five whitetails. Of them, two were trophy-class bucks lost to tidal-marshland swamps and sudden rainstorms. It is just not worth all the problems. Hunt for pleasure, not misery. Stay home in bed like other animals in nature do and hunt right after the rain ends, which is always the best time to hunt deer!

The ascending full moon during the months of October, November, and December, etc., is the controlling factor that causes the doe's estrous cycle to occur every twenty-six to twenty-eight days. Most hunters who are now just learning to understand this natural phenomenon would probably assume that hunting deer during the time of the full moon would prove to be very productive. It can be, if you know why and when, otherwise you could be just wasting your time!

During the days of the full moon, most deer return to their daytime beds well before daylight and leave their beds near or after dark. Generally, most deer have bedded down for the day well before most hunters ever arrive at the woods in the early morning hours to hunt them, and most hunters leave the woods at dark, well before most deer naturally rise and leave their daytime beds. The best time of day to hunt deer during the full moon is between the hours of ten a.m. and two p.m. Especially during the primary rut, when the mature bucks of the herd travel around their home range areas on their scent trails checking the condition of their rubs and scrapes, while all of the does of the herd are bedding down for the day. Then in the later afternoon, the bucks bed down somewhere downwind of the herd's master scrape, near the does' bedding areas. They wait there until the does leave their beds, near or after dark.

During the days of the full moon the does of the herd sometimes leave their daytime beds for nibbles of food or water near mid-day. They have been bedded down since before daylight, much earlier than usual, chewing their cuds and sleeping on and off, and it is usually just about the normal period of time for them to stretch their legs, maybe get some water, and relieve themselves of their bodily waste. When the does randomly, temporarily leave and return to their various daytime bedding areas near mid-day, during the rut the very anxious, ready-to-mate, mature bucks naturally follow after them. These nervous,

The author believes that the controversial "going away shot" is actually a very good shot for a skilled archer.

breeding bucks will be constantly traveling back and forth between the various bedding areas, checking for any doe in estrous that may have traveled anywhere near their scrapes or the herd's master scrape in the same area of the herd's home range territory. This is one reason why whitetail bucks lose much of their body weight during the rut, and this is why you should be hunting from ten a.m. to two p.m. during the days of the full moon. This is usually the only time of the day that a whitetail deer will be traveling around in daylight during the full moon under natural conditions! This is also why you should never plan a hunt anywhere, for any big game animal, during the full moon, unless it is the mating season for that particular animal, and you plan to hunt that animal during mid-day. Otherwise you are just wasting your time and energy!

If the sky was totally overcast during the entire period of the full moon, the clouds would block the moon's bright light from the fields and woods at night. The deer would react to the lower than normal light levels on the land, as they would on any other cloudy day and they would leave their daytime beds much earlier in the afternoon and return to their beds much later in the morning. Except for this one condition, you usually will not see any deer or many other animals traveling around in daylight during the full moon, unless some other hunter or something else caused them to move!

While you are hunting in the woods, listen to the birds and insects all around the area that you are hunting, as they will warn you when something is coming near or traveling through the woods off in the distance. When you hear a blue jay, a crow, or woodpeckers call out, or see groups of small birds that are feeding nearby suddenly take flight, or hear the chirping of crickets or other insects suddenly stop and become quiet, something is definitely moving around in the woods. It could be a deer feeding, a fox running, a human walking, etc. Regardless, be alert; something has definitely disturbed them. Their calls or signs of alarm and the barking of the chipmunks and squirrels also serve to warn the deer and other animals when a human hunter is walking in the woods, or makes too much noise moving around. In fact, any fast movements of your arms or hands, or any uncovered skin on your face and hands shining in the sun would be enough to alert most animals and birds of your presence, which could quite possibly ruin your hunting chances in that area for the day.

CHAPTER THIRTEEN

RIGHT PLACE, RIGHT TIME, RIGHT DEER

If you plan to hunt near a deer herd's bedding area in the morning you should try to time your arrival at your hunting location in the woods about two hours after sunrise. Most deer will not usually arrive at their bedding areas until about three hours after sunrise, depending on weather conditions. Many times hunters will arrive too early in the morning to hunt near a deer herd's bedding area before the thermal reversal occurs. Most of the time these hunters are only broadcasting their scent and their hunting location to the deer when the deer circle out around somewhere downwind of their bedding areas while feeding in the early morning hours. You would probably see more deer if you slowly still-hunt your way through the woods toward the deer's bedding areas at sunrise, moving and traveling slow, than you would slamming a climbing, portable treestand up against a tree ten to fifteen times in the dark morning hours for all the deer in the woods to hear.

If you plan to hunt in the woods or near a deer herd's bedding area in the late afternoon, you should plan to be at your hunting location at least three hours before sundown. Otherwise, you will probably be walking through areas of the open woods disturbing the birds and other small animals feeding at a time when most deer are leaving, or have already left their daytime beds. This is not a very good time of day for you to be walking around in the open woods if you want to kill a deer. Deer are very alert to conditions in the woods when they leave their daytime beds and begin traveling out through the open woods toward their feeding areas. Any disturbance anywhere in the herd's home range territory would cause the deer to shift their normal travels far downwind.

Being at your hunting location in the woods three hours before sunset does not necessarily mean that you will see the herd's bucks traveling around at this time of day. They will naturally follow later on in time, if you allow the family groups and the other less dominant deer to pass by you undisturbed. If you cannot be at your hunting location in the woods three hours before sunset, you should plan to hunt the deer somewhere near their feeding areas, rather than disturbing the woods and spooking the deer.

If you plan to hunt in the woods near the edge of crop fields in the late afternoon, you should be at your hunting location at least two hours before sundown, and you should hunt the side of the field where the wind or thermal flows out of the woods to the field. The deer will be traveling from their bedding areas with the wind or thermal to their backs and quartering off their backs, and they will usually enter the crop field from the woods with the wind or thermals to their backs or quartering off their backs. If you plan to hunt deer near crop fields, or somewhere between the crop fields and the deer's bedding area in the early morning hours, you should be at your hunting position at least fifteen minutes before daylight.

Regardless of where you are hunting in the morning or the late afternoon, you should always try to time your arrival at your hunting location close to when the thermal reversal occurs. Once again, deer leave their daytime beds

Thanks to superb management the whitetail deer exists in millions . . . but the author feels more areas should be managed for trophy quality so there are more mature bucks in the herd and youngsters like this get a chance to grow up.

after the thermal reversal occurs in the late afternoon, and deer return to their daytime bedding areas after the thermal reversal occurs in the morning, depending on the weather conditions. Whenever possible, you should always try to approach any deer bedding area, a master scrape, or your treestand or ground blind location by walking a straight-line path directly to the area, using a stalking stick, and approaching from a crosswind direction, meaning you keep the thermal or wind flowing to the side of your face or with the wind in your face. By doing so, you create much less disturbance in and around the area you plan to hunt for the deer to detect. Too much kicked up, fresh ground scent in the air in any particular area of the woods, would be out of place, and it would definitely alert the deer when they traveled near the area. Approaching any area from a crosswind direction or with the wind in your face, will help you prevent the deer from hearing or scenting you from downwind, and it will also help keep you out of the deer's direct front field of vision as you approach. Remember, deer normally bed and travel with the wind or thermals to their backs or quartering off their backs.

As I mentioned earlier, deer are colorblind. However, they can definitely see the very apparent, iridescent, "fuzzy glow" of the highly visible, "fluorescent orange" hunting clothing. If orange is required, I would highly recommend that you use the hunter orange clothing in some type of a camouflaged pattern where legal, instead of the glowing solid fluorescent orange clothing, or the deer and other animals will definitely see you.

Not all areas contain big, large-racked trophy bucks. It mostly all depends on the area of the country, the available food sources, the elements in the soil, hunting pressure, and the subspecies of whitetail deer that live in the area of the country that you are hunting. There are many subspecies of whitetail deer. Some of the main differences separating most of the subspecies from one another are the variations of hair color on each deer's muzzle, or on their body or legs, or how far the white belly hair extends up the body, or their geographic location, etc. Most of these subspecies were erroneously separated and misnamed because of minor variations of hair color that may

Even if buck seasons were closed on a rotational basis to let bucks grow up and close up the buck/doe ratios trophies like this would not be easy to hunt . . . but there would be more of them!

have naturally occurred as the result of adaptation to a local environment or breeding. Most hunters need only concern themselves with two basic subspecies: the "*borealis*" and the "*virginianus*."

The *borealis* are the largest of the whitetail deer and they are generally found throughout the provinces of Canada and most of the mid-northern regions of the United States. Mature bucks normally grow to body weights of well over 200 pounds, with mature does weighing 120 to 150 pounds. These big *borealis* whitetails usually carry big, heavy, thick antlers that match their body size, and their tracks and droppings are generally much bigger than those of their southern cousins.

The *virginianus* subspecies of whitetail deer are generally found in most of the eastern United States and throughout the South. The average doe weighs approximately ninty pounds; the average buck approximately 135 pounds. Many bucks of the *virginianus* subspecies carry fine racks, but most are usually smaller than those of the northern whitetails. However, there are always exceptions.

I have seen well over 100 whitetail deer in one day on many different occasions while bowhunting in the mountainous regions of the George Washington National Forest in West Virginia. I have also seen just as many deer while bow hunting in other various "public hunting areas" located throughout Maryland, Pennsylvania, New York, and Virginia. The whitetail deer are plentiful in many of these areas, thanks to highly successful wildlife management programs developed by these states in the past and present day, the abundance of natural foods, and God. However, in my opinion, many of these current wildlife management programs should be modified to enhance the number of mature, trophy bucks by rotating a "no kill" buck season in certain areas or counties for three years at a time, which would allow more young bucks to grow to physical maturity. In many areas, the doe to buck ratios are as high as twenty-five to thirty-five does to one mature buck, much too skewed. My "rotation plan" would not really affect any of the hunters who are out hunting for the meat, and some trophy hunters may have to travel farther to get their buck. But for most hunters it would be well worth the wait and the temporary extra traveling time to know that there would be true, trophy-class whitetail bucks in those areas when buck season returned after the three-year moratorium.

Generally, the farther south you travel from anywhere

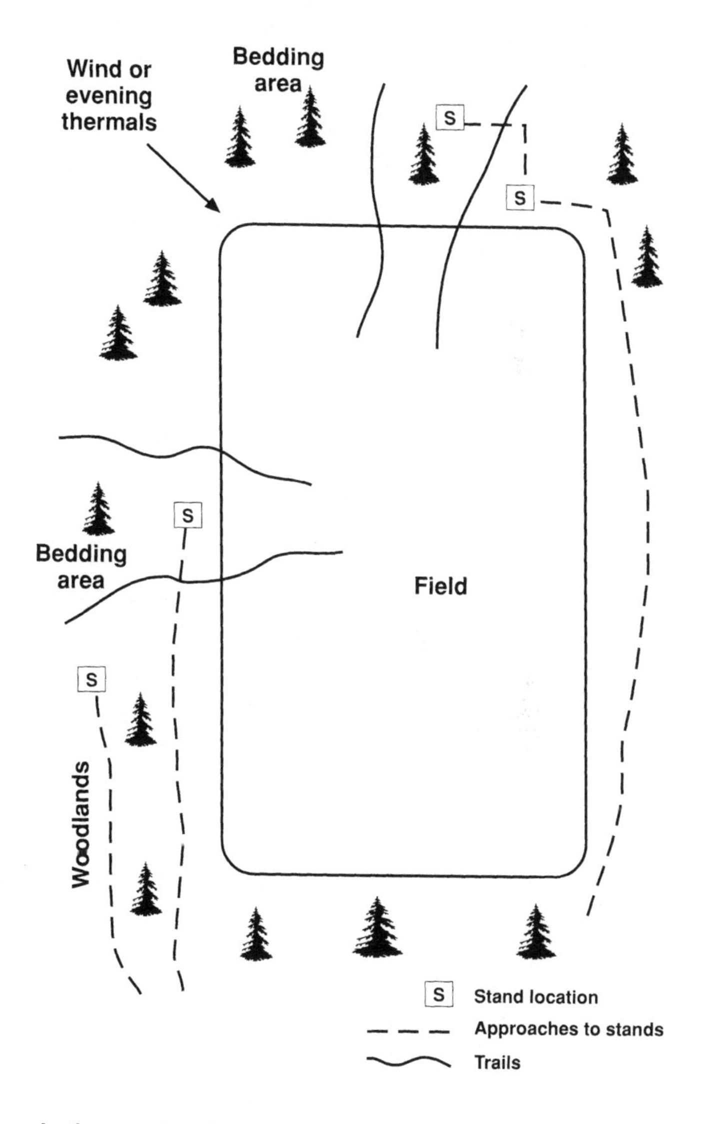

In the evening deer enter feeding areas with the wind or thermals to their backs or quartering off their backs. Try to be on stand three hours before sunset.

along the Canadian border, the smaller deer are, excepting small herds of *borealis* whitetail deer found in and around some of the major farmbelt areas and other naturally rich soil areas of our country. Many of these northern deer were transplanted into these areas in the past to help revitalize depleted deer herds that were once hunted to near extinction in some states, while others were naturally dispersed to other areas by evolution and extreme hunting pressure.

The melting of glaciers during the Ice Age created great water flows that shaped the land and terrain of North America. These flowing waters eroded the earth's surface, which produced mountain valleys and river drainage systems, and as a result, flooding waters deposited sediment into various areas of our country. These areas usually contain the best soil conditions and produce the best natural food plants which in turn produce larger animals of the same species. They eat better natural foods, so they grow faster and larger than other members of their species.

Unless you have plenty of money and lots of time to travel to various areas and states of our country and Canada to hunt for larger bodied, bigger-antlered deer, you are economically forced to hunt in an area near where you live. There might not be giant-bodied whitetails in your hunting areas, but there are deer, and mature bucks to hunt. I have killed with bow and arrow twenty-seven well-documented whitetail bucks that have dressed out at over 200 pounds—hunting in and around various public hunting areas and some private lands where large, trophy-class whitetail bucks were not thought to exist. However, I don't hunt like most other hunters!

It is true that most all of my whitetail experience is associated with bowhunting and with deer behavior that is typical of the terrain and forests of the eastern United States and Canada. However, after recent visits to Idaho, Montana,

There are almost always a few big bucks around; the author has taken many bucks like this from areas where trophy bucks were thought not to exist. Dressing out at 203 pounds, this buck scored 148 6/8 P&Y.

and Wyoming—plus some midwestern states—I have found that the behavior of the whitetail deer is pretty much the same there as anywhere else they are found. I did learn that western whitetails, who are dominated by the larger elk, moose, and mule deer for food and habitat, are naturally forced to live in and around certain isolated areas. And they are generally hunted much less than their eastern cousins. This is mainly due to the very low number of human hunters out there, vast wilderness areas, and the abundance of the larger, more impressive elk and generally more available mule deer being the preferred game animals.

As one experienced resident big-game trophy hunter I met out West and stayed with for a while put it, "Why would any trophy hunter want to hunt smaller-bodied, smaller-antlered whitetail when there are so many monstrous elk and mule deer to hunt?" After seeing some of those big boys walking around out there I don't argue the point. For those of you who have the money and the time to travel to any of those western states or western Canada—if you know where to go—there are plenty of trophy-class whitetail bucks out there that are virtually unhunted in some of that vast, beautiful country.

In the writing of this book I have tried to simply explain the complex life of a truly remarkable animal that has the ability to adapt to most any situation or environment. This book is not based on theories or trends, but on scientific evidence and the life experience of a man who has spent many years of his life in the woods studying the natural behavior of whitetail deer—and bowhunting them—as a profession. In closing, I offer this advice: This is a time when most deer hunters of today are carrying all types of lures, calls, rattling antlers, decoys, timers, and such into the heavily hunted woods of the eastern United States. It seems quite obvious to me that a hunter who understands deer behavior, who hunts cleanly and quietly, and puts to good advantage what nature grows in the woods, also has a definite advantage over other hunters—and also over the whitetail deer.

CHAPTER FOURTEEN

LEARN THE LESSON

Many human hunters of today's world ride to their tree stands or their favorite hunting grounds on their ATV's (All Terrain Vehicles) guided by their GPS's (Global Positioning Systems). Many purchase and wear very expensive, scent eliminating hunting clothing with a very specific camouflage pattern, and they carry the fastest bows or the most powerful hunting firearms ever known to mankind. They also spend many uncounted hours of their spare time watching hunting channel programs on television or viewing rented, purchased or borrowed video tapes on hunting deer. Yet, they still do not kill a deer every season, year after year, much less a trophy buck. What is wrong with these people? Do they think that the deer are blind and stupid? Do they fully understand how Whitetail deer really live and survive in the real world? I truly believe that many hunters do not realize that a mature Whitetail deer is a very smart animal. The actual hunting and killing of a deer is probably the closest psychological experience there is to hunting a human being in combat, except the deer don't carry any weapons. They can evade you. They can escape you, and they are able to learn from your and other human beings' bad hunting habits.

I have taken well over four hundred Whitetail deer hunting solely with the bow and arrow. I have also taken twelve Black Bear, seven Moose, and hundreds of other small game, wild turkeys, grouse, ducks, etc., hunting solely with bow and arrows. I spent over eighteen years of my life working in the woods studying the Natural Behavior of the Whitetail Deer while employed by the Smithsonian Institution at an environmental research center. I have read and reviewed just about every article or study ever published in the various scientific journals about the Whitetail deer and their behavior. I have trapped, tagged, and released wild deer. I have stayed out all night, during the full moon, many times over many years just to observe wild Whitetail deer behavior during the rut and other mating cycles at night when they are normally the most active. I have stalked in towards, and killed many Whitetail bucks while they were sleeping in their beds, while their heads were still bobbing up and down in sleep. I have blood trailed hundreds of deer and other big animals. I have clocked Whitetail deer running flat out at fifty miles per hour, and I have seen deer swim across two miles of open water just to feed. I have seen deer run up a steep, half mile long, sixty-five degree rocky incline just to escape a human hunter a quarter of a mile away. I am here to tell you that Whitetail deer are very smart animals, and very human smart. Especially if they have managed to survive past their first year and a half of life and at least one hunting season.

Though most of my hunting experience is with the bow and arrow, most every year I would also hunt the Whitetail deer during the various firearms seasons of many different states with the bow and arrow, and I have usually killed a nice buck on the first morning of the first day of hunting. As I hunted with the bow and arrow during these many past firearms hunting seasons, I have always observed the activities of the many firearms hunters in the woods near and around the areas where I was hunting. Many were loud talkers and flashlight shiners. I have heard and watched other hunters as they drove their noisy, puttering ATV's through the fields and woods with lights on. I have also seen many other hunters drive their hunting vehicles with loud, pounding mufflers into various woodlots and fields, shining their headlights into their hunting areas and slamming their vehicles doors shut just before heading out towards the woods to hunt. Some of these same hunters have walked up to me while I was field dressing my deer, usually greeting me with, "nice buck, I didn't even see a doe this morning". Most of these hunters really have no clue that their actions alone have spooked many of the deer away from their hunting areas into deep cover or other distant areas.

During many past firearms hunting seasons, I would purposely walk deep into the woods with my bow and arrows the night before the opening morning. I would spend the night sleeping in the deep woods waiting for daylight, and the arrival of the human hunters. I planned to use the arrival and entry of many firearm hunters, and all the noise and disturbance associated with all those hunters entering the fringe areas, all around the deeps woods where I spent the night, to push or drive the deer towards me. This method of ambush and hunting has worked for me many times and almost always provided me with a fine, mature Whitetail buck to drag out of the woods. Most hunters would have never thought of hunting for trophy deer this way. But, I do!

In rural areas, it is not unusual for many firearm hunters to go out to where they are actually going to hunt, usually on family or friends of family lands, to test fire their hunting rifles or to check the accuracy of their rifle scope a week or a day before hunting season opens. In many cases it is actually a yearly tradition! Most of these people do not even realize that all the shooting of high power rifles, in and around the areas where they plan to hunt, is going to drive most of the mature deer far from that area, and cause most of the other local deer to become extremely nocturnal.

Many other hunters drive to out of state hunting grounds, two or three days prior to the opening day of hunting season, and they walk or drive their ATV's all over and through the woods where they plan to hunt, scouting for deer sign and locations to put up their climbing treestands. Most of these types of hunters also have no idea that they, themselves, are driving most of the deer far from their hunting area, and forcing the deer to become even more nocturnal than they normally are. Most of these hunters seem to believe that the deer will simply forget about all the commotion and disturbance in the woods, and to their lives. They seem to expect that the deer will immediately return back to their normal feeding and traveling routines.

ATV's are great utility vehicles and they are very useful tools to help hunters recover downed game from very remote areas of the woods and mountains. ATV's also provide the means for some hunters to travel deep into wilderness areas to hunt big game where not many other hunters have easily ventured before. However, most hunters abuse the use of ATV's while hunting by traveling all over and through the very woods they plan to hunt, time and time again, weekend after weekend, before and during all the hunting seasons. All the loud, puttering noises and bright lights shining through the woods as hunters enter and travel to their favorite hunting grounds, treestands, etc., spooks the deer and other animals that live in the woods. Most modern hunters need only to view the old Walt Disney movie or current video version of *Bambi* to understand how most animals react to human hunters entering their world on foot, much less hunters driving around through the woods on their ATV's.

A hunter who needs to use an ATV for remote hunting purposes would do well to have a much quieter muffler system and low level, night lighting installed on their ATV to help spook less game at greater distances away. Manufacturers originally designed and built most ATV's to function as utility vehicles to be used on farms, etc., where minimal noise control and low level lighting were not the main design criteria. Since most of the ATV's currently being sold are primarily sold to hunters for thousands of dollars each, it is time for hunters to tell the manufacturers to design and build quiet ATV's specifically for hunting!

Generally, in heavily hunted areas, if a firearms hunter does not kill a buck or any deer within the first two or three days of the firearms season, the odds are really against that hunter even seeing or killing a deer. Because most of the other deer living in that area will have become extremely nocturnal once a few loud rifle shots sound out in the early morning woods on the opening morning. The only effective way to hunt these spooked deer now is for hunters, or dogs where legal, to jump up the deer and drive them out and away from their beds in thick cover areas. Hopefully towards other hunters waiting in ambush some distance away.

Many deer killed by the majority of hunters during the first couple of days of most firearms seasons have been driven away from other distant woods by other hunters entering and leaving those woods to hunt. This usually occurs each day as hunters enter and leave the woods during the early morning hours, before and after lunch, and early to late afternoon. Simply stated, hunters pushing deer towards other hunters. This is one reason why successful hunting for trophy bucks during most firearms seasons in large public hunting areas is considered by many to be more luck rather than skill. And, this is why I have always walked deep into the woods with my bow and arrows the night before the opening morning of most firearms seasons. I used all the other hunters entering the woods all around me at daylight to push and drive the deer towards me in the deep woods, where I was waiting in ambush. I always considered this simple maneuver to be quite skillful!

In the state of West Virginia, where I currently live, the baiting of deer is legal. Many hunters haul in truckloads of apples or corn into various fields and woodlots. They build permanent treestands or tree houses complete with heaters and windows, thirty to forty yards away from the bait pile, and they shoot any deer that ever approaches or feeds at the bait pile. To many people this is deer hunting! Most of the deer that ever approach these types of baited food areas during daylight conditions are generally the young deer of the herd, usually less than a year and a half in age. Most of the people that hunt deer this way state that they really do not care if they kill a trophy buck or not, they just want to kill a deer. If an occasional small antlered buck happens to follow an immature doe to the food pile, so much the better. It's a trophy deer to them!

Occasionally, these types of hunters may kill an immature buck or so, over a period of a few years, but most really believe that there are no large mature bucks around because they never see them at their apple piles. A mature Whitetail buck would almost never walk into a baited food pile under daylight conditions, if at all. It is totally out of place, and it means danger to them! Their previous life experiences with many different human hunters over past hunting seasons have taught them to stay far away from the scent of humans found all around these types of baited areas. A mature Whitetail buck may chase or follow a doe in estrous or heat near or through a baited food area or food plot well after dark on occasion, but that would be rare.

As I have mentioned before, mature Whitetail bucks almost never travel around in daylight conditions, except during the periods of time when the does are in estrous or heat, or when they have been jumped up and driven from their daytime beds by some natural predator or a human hunter. This is one reason why most trophy Whitetail bucks are hard to hunt, and why they survive most human hunters. The does will continuously cycle back into estrous or heat, each month, near the rising full moon from October through March, as long as they have not been successfully bred. I discovered these and many other amazing facts about the Whitetail deer's life during my behavioral studies.

Most poachers, road hunters, and other people who have baited in deer with apples or corn for years and have only killed young bucks or other immature deer have all learned to wait until well after dark to begin their idea of hunting. Many fine Whitetail bucks are killed each year illegally by poachers spotlighting the deer well after dark, before, during and after most firearms hunting seasons. In my opinion, there are probably half as many unchecked, illegally killed Whitetail bucks and does taken by poachers, road hunters, etc., as there are deer legally harvested by most conscientious law-abiding hunters.

Most states purposely schedule their main firearm hunting seasons to occur after the doe's second estrous cycle, the deer's main breeding period or rut, to ensure that many of the does have been bred before many of the mature breeding bucks are killed by firearms hunters. The remainders of the does are usually bred during their continuing monthly estrous cycles through March by any surviving mature bucks. Some of my success hunting trophy Whitetail bucks with the bow and arrows was due to the fact that I was able to hunt all the breeding cycles of the does from

October through January in many different areas and states. I was able to hunt mature Whitetail bucks before, during, and long after most firearms hunting seasons had ended. A time of the year when very few human hunters are in the woods, and a time of the year when most deer have somewhat returned to their normal behavior and movement patterns.

Much of my success hunting deer, bear, moose, wild turkeys, etc., is due to the fact that I hunt much differently than most other human hunters. I do not go hunting just because it is the opening day of the season. I do not take a week off from life to go hunting just because it is the first week of the hunting season. I let the weather, the winds and daylight conditions determine how, when and where I hunt. I mostly hunt from natural ground blinds, atop large mountain rocks, or I will hastily build a ground blind from natural materials to hunt a particular area or location. I promptly head to the woods to hunt right after a rain or snow storm ends, or right after a dramatic change in the direction of the wind. If a rain or snow storm ends or the wind suddenly shifts out of a different direction, I go to the woods to hunt right then. I do not wait for the weekend to arrive to go hunting. I go when the time is right! I air out all my hunting clothing and equipment daily. I use natural cover scents whenever possible to help mask my natural body odor and equipment scent. I never use flashlights in the woods except for an occasional after-dark blood trailing or field dressing. I will sometimes use a portable treestand to hunt, but I would rarely ever use a permanent treestand to hunt any big game animal. I use to my advantage anything I can to make my hunt the most productive.

Once again, I use a stalking stick whenever I enter the woods or travel through the woods when I hunt any species of big game. When I first began my studies of the Natural

Behavior of Wild Whitetail Deer, my initial problem was to figure out a way to get close enough to wild deer to study their behavior. I served in an Infantry Recon Unit in the Viet Nam War. I had successfully completed Jungle Warfare Training, Survival, and many other military combat training courses. The military taught me how to hunt humans very well. During hundreds of daytime and nighttime ambush patrols, hunting other human beings, I attained a unique skill of determining the number of enemy present by the sounds created by their feet and gait while they were approaching and walking through various kill zone areas. I was also an excellent tracker of the human enemy! I learned that humans have a very distinct, two step, walking pattern. Since most all animals living in the woods travel around on four legs, I surmised that most human beings walking through woods on two legs would easily be detected by most animals because the sounds of a human's walking gait was just too much out of place in the woods. It spooked the animals.

One day, near the beginning of my behavioral studies. I carried a walking stick into the woods with me, and used the walking stick to create a walking type sound in between each normal step I took with my feet, to simulate the rhythm and sounds of a four legged animal walking in the woods. As I entered various study areas in the undisturbed woods, traveling with the wind to my face. I walked, unnoticed, right up to a few different family groups of deer sleeping in their daytime beds. That day, I learned the importance of what I now call my "stalking stick", and I have used it ever since to get in close enough to wild Whitetail deer to study their behavior, and to hunt and stalk to within bow shooting range of deer, bear, moose, etc. The use of the stalking stick is one of the most important hunting lessons that I can pass on to other hunters!

Many modern hunters seem to believe that if they just buy the right hunting clothes, the most powerful hunting rifle, the best ATV, and the most popular hunting calls and lures on the market. The deer will just run right up to them and stand broadside, perfectly still for them to shoot and kill. They watch videotapes on their televisions showing some specific deer behavior that may have been filmed many times in game preserves and edited with dialogs created to fit any given situation to sell a specific idea or product. Many hunters believe what they see in these, what I call, "Hollywood Hunting Videos" to be the Whitetail deer's true natural behavior, and they hunt deer accordingly. These are just some of the many reasons why the majority of hunters do not see or kill trophy Whitetail bucks. They just do not understand how Whitetail deer really live and survive, and they do not know how to enter and leave the deer's world without being detected by the deer.

Just about everything concerning the Whitetail deer has been observed, studied, over studied and published. There is really nothing new to be learned about the Whitetail deer that would benefit the average deer hunter's success rate of bringing home the meat. I wrote this book in a very condensed, yet simple to read format to enlighten people and hunters how deer generally live and survive in their simple, yet very predictable world. If there is something about the Whitetail deer that you do not understand, read this book again, but this time do not skip a page. If you become slightly confused about such items as, how deer use the winds or thermals, reread those sections of the book before you continue on. As with any other subject matter there are always going to be some exceptions to the rules of normal Whitetail deer behavior. There are always going to be some circumstances or situations where a particular deer's behavior varies from what I have described to you as normal behavior. And, there is always going to be a "Mr. Joe Hunter" who saw a deer doing something totally different than normal. Neither I nor any other man alive could possibly answer every hunting question or cover every deer behavior situation in a single book. But, at least if you understand how most deer generally live and react to certain situations, ninety per cent of the time. The odds of probability and success are in your favor. Learn the lesson!

INDEX

Note: Bold page numbers indicate illustrations or photos.